Praise for *Leadership Requires Ex*

"Ritch Eich has a passion for the study of leaders... ...p. in *Leadership Requires Extra Innings*, Ritch explores how successful leaders create high performance teams capable of accomplishing great things. I recommend this book to anyone who wants to take their leadership competencies to the next level!"

—David A. Brandon, Donald R. Shepherd Director of Intercollegiate Athletics, University of Michigan, and former chairman and CEO, Domino's Pizza

"Ritch Eich has a magical ability—turning the impossible into the possible—as his numerous career accomplishments clearly reveal. At Pomona, Blue Shield, Stanford, the Navy, California Lutheran University and now with his second book, his rich experiences will be available to all. Ritch is a leader's leader."

—William Kearney, senior vice president, Merrill Lynch

"Successful leadership necessarily warrants respect for, and consideration of, all stakeholder interests. Ritch Eich understands this foundational maxim and encourages those in positions of leadership and those aspiring to lead to elicit feedback from others affected by operational decisions and parlay those ideas into meaningful and sustainable action."

—Elizabeth F. R. Gingerich, editor-in-chief, *Journal of Values-Based Leadership*

"Ritch Eich does a masterful job of sharing his wisdom and lifelong leadership insights. The book is an instant classic."

—Noel M. Tichy, bestselling coauthor of *Judgment, The Leadership Engine,* and *Control Your Destiny or Someone Else Will*

Praise for Ritch's First Book *Real Leaders Don't Boss*

The author's royalties from sales of Real Leaders Don't Boss *are being donated to not-for-profit organizations caring for veterans wounded in Iraq and Afghanistan.*

"Ritch Eich's leadership style is part Warren Bennis and Max DePree, part John Greenleaf and Peter Drucker, and part Jackie Robinson and Colin Powell. Ritch is a change agent and has worked tirelessly to transform the management practices and processes he inherited in each of his positions of increasing responsibility. As a leadership and management consultant, Ritch is continuing to share 'best practices' from the leadership field."

—Steve Grafton, president and CEO, The University of Michigan Alumni Association

"*Real Leaders Don't Boss* is a 'can't miss' leadership book. Ritch wouldn't write anything less."

—Senator Richard Lugar, Senate Foreign Relations Committee

"Ritch Eich is a man of experience. The best leaders are the ones who have taken the high road and now can lift others. Ritch is that leader."

—Rich DeVos, cofounder, Amway Corporation, and owner, Orlando Magic, NBA

"He has demonstrated the ability to lead from the front and also from the back...he knows what true leadership is about and has pulled it off in the heat of battle. No stranger to adversity, Ritch has proven time and time again how to bounce back and succeed where others would have given up."

—Rear Admiral William Thompson (ret.), US Navy, former Chief of Information, Pentagon, Department of the Navy, and founding president of the US Navy Memorial, Washington, DC

"Ritch Eich's work career began in the California peach orchards of Sutter and Yuba Counties. Raised by parents who were teachers and community volunteers, he developed a keen appreciation for inclusion and diversity early in life. Ritch has been placed in the top marketing and public relations posts. In each executive role, he has been a most effective change agent and transformational leader. Despite his success from humble beginnings, he retains his modesty, balance, and deep concern for others less fortunate. Nearly a year ago, he embarked on a long-held dream to launch his own marketing and strategy consulting firm and write a book on leadership. *Real Leaders Don't Boss* is a 'must read.'"

—Harold Edwards, president and CEO, Limoneira Company

"Most books on leadership are not worth reading because they are long on the theory of leadership, but miss the heart of leadership. *Real Leaders Don't Boss* is an important exception. If you are interested in the 'whys' and 'hows' of leadership, get a copy, snag a couple of hours to read it, and you will have the insights you need to be the leader you have always wanted to be."

—Robert A. Sevier, PhD, senior vice president, Stamats, Inc.

Leadership

REQUIRES

EXTRA
INNINGS

Lessons on Leading from a Life in the Trenches

Ritch K. Eich, PhD

No part of this publication may be reproduced, stored in a retrieval system, or transmitted in any form or by any means, electronic, mechanical, photocopying, recording, scanning, or otherwise, except as permitted under Section 107 or 108 of the 1976 United States Copyright Act, without the prior written permission of the Author. To request permission or for additional information, please refer to www.eichassociated.com

Editorial and project management:
Second City Publishing Services LLC.
www.secondcitypublishing.com

Printed in the United States of America

www.eichassociated.com
ISBN: 978-0-615-86107-4

Copyright © 2013 Ritch K. Eich, PhD. All rights reserved.

DEDICATION

*"A life is not important except in the impact it has
on other lives."*

—*Jackie Robinson*

This book is dedicated to the legacy of my childhood
hero, Jackie Robinson. Proceeds from its sale will be
donated to The Jackie Robinson Foundation, a national
not-for-profit organization founded by Jackie's widow,
Rachel Robinson.

Through the Foundation, Jackie's family and the legion
of their friends and admirers are perpetuating his
courage, caring, and commitment to creating a better
life for all people every day.

CONTENTS

Contents

PREFACE

The term "extra innings" refers to the continuation of a tie game beyond the normal nine innings played by baseball teams. While some believe the outcome of most tie games is a result of pure luck, I think they are more attributable to the following learned leadership lessons: preparation, including conditioning that builds endurance and durability while minimizing injury; desire, including a hunger and yearning to achieve success; a strong bench and bullpen; the ability to come through in critical moments (the clutch); cohesion among players accompanied by an unshakable belief in the team—and last, but not least, skill.

As we all know, nothing in life is a sure thing, except death and taxes. During a lifetime of working in agriculture, hospitals, academe, and the military, I have learned first-hand that leadership success often requires "extra innings." There are no shortcuts to becoming a great leader, but the journey can be incredible. In this book, I've compiled a collection of essays that span my own journey over the course of more than

30 years of working with CEOs, coaches, military personnel, healthcare professionals, and others.

Leaders, like followers, are unique individuals. By no means do all leaders reside in the C-suite. And, there is no single definition of what makes a leader effective, but there are similarities they all share. Leaders know they can't lead by themselves. There's no doubt that a lot of the leaders I have known have healthy egos, but they also know that they can't be leaders if they don't have followers. And you can't have followers if you don't set an example that people want to follow.

I love all kinds of sports; I participated in them during high school and college and follow them to this day. There are a lot of lessons leaders can learn from coaches. The best coaches understand that the goal isn't just to win—it's also helping team members become champions off the field as well. Coaches understand that players can learn from both the outstanding and not-so-outstanding players. Leaders understand this as well.

I learned early in life that leaders don't just press for change—they also do the heavy lifting and mundane tasks. Leaders inspire those with whom they work by setting the right example. They never ask others to do what they cannot or will not do. They know their team members' strengths, weaknesses, and career aspirations regardless of whether those team members are located in the home office or at some remote site accessible only by bush plane. They take the time to visit with them regularly, remembering names and significant information about them— matters that are important to those individuals. Leaders are humble, but passionate. The best leaders teach others how they themselves conquered adversity and coped with failure. Failing is a very valuable experience, and it is how you deal with failure and bounce back that provide the vital learning skills.

As I was putting the finishing touches on this book, several people came to mind I believe anybody would be extremely fortunate to have with them in a ferocious storm, or in the middle of a business crisis.

Dr. Carol "TK" Tomlinson-Keasey was the founding chancellor of the newest of the University of California campuses, UC Merced. Despite insurmountable odds both professional and personal, Dr. TK persevered. Dr. Laurine (Betty) Fitzgerald of Michigan State University was one of the most intelligent people I've ever known. A true renaissance woman, Dr. Fitzgerald was never ever afraid to get her hands dirty and help prepare students for the real world. Verena Kloos of the BMW Group is one of the leading women in the global auto industry. These three women stand as beacons of intelligence, high performance, grace under pressure, and class in what was once a male-dominated business world. While these highly skilled women have broken through the glass ceiling, more needs to be done to ensure gender equality.

Finally, Les Palm and Dave Francis are two very good friends and terrific athletes from elementary school on. I highlighted Les in my first book, *Real Leaders Don't Boss*. Dave and I went to Sacramento State together, where Dave played football while I played tennis. After graduation, Dave taught and coached in junior high, high school, and college and now lives in Shingle Springs, California. Gary Ames, another very good friend from Marysville, California, is a Purple Heart and Silver Star recipient recognized for valor in Vietnam for saving the lives of his platoon. My sons, Geoff and Ted Eich, continue to amaze me. Geoff, a Marine Harrier pilot, courageously flew combat missions in Iraq and Afghanistan, and Ted served two tours in exemplary fashion in the Persian Gulf as a navy "ship driver" enforcing United Nations sanctions and antiterrorism efforts. Geoff is an executive director at Amgen and Ted is an attorney with PwC (PricewaterhouseCoopers). All of these persons are outstanding examples of leaders who have inspired me.

Because there are many more essays than will fit in one volume, I have chosen to focus on the ones that I feel will have the most impact on you. They are all deliberately short, and designed to be easily digested during a daily commute or a few hours on a plane. I have no doubt that after reading this book, you will have discovered some ideas that you can integrate into your own style of leadership right away. I've had the privilege to work with— and learn from—many people throughout my career, including some well-known leaders. I love to name names and provide credit where credit is due. My "name dropping" throughout the book is not intended to impress readers with who I know but rather to acknowledge that leadership is an acquired skill. Being prepared for the unexpected, an invaluable leadership capability, can be learned in different ways.

Leadership is both an art and a science, and something that can be mastered if you are truly committed to improving your skills. Experiences of very different kinds and in very different settings are not just great teachers, they are the best way to become a leader. People ranging from my father—a teacher, coach, and school principal—to the CEO of Jiffy Mix have inspired me. You'll meet all of these folks in this book. You'll learn about leadership from groups as diverse as the US Marine Corps and college marching bands.

Results matter but so do relationships. Leaders focus on long-term results, not just quarterly profits. Leaders respect, appreciate, and allow people to be individuals. They demand excellence and provide autonomy. Leaders know the importance of establishing a reservoir of goodwill to help them when the going gets tough—they know crises will occur, people will make mistakes, and others will find fault with their decisions.

One of the main weaknesses of organizations is not looking to the future and instead focusing only on the present. This is exaggerated when economies are in difficult straits, budgets are tight, and layoffs often require people to take over jobs that were once done by two or three people. The best organizations have a cache of internally developed leaders who understand the company's business strategy along with its culture—people who possess the internal credibility to drive meaningful change and quality performance.

One of the people who taught me about the importance of always looking to the future was my college tennis coach Jack Jossi, a master of strategy and anticipation. He won the Pacific Coast Tennis Championships at age 19 and was a highly ranked amateur. After he turned pro, Jack traveled with such tennis immortals as Bill Tilden, Don Budge, Fred Perry, Bobby Riggs, and Frank Kovacs. As a freshman playing singles and doubles on the Sacramento State Hornets varsity team, I had never seen anyone hit a tennis ball so many different ways with so many different types of spin. He made sure that all of us played our upcoming matches in our heads well before the actual match— he taught us to focus on the future, not just the present. As a result of his leadership, we were able to dominate the Far Western Conference in the 60s.

Leaders have a primary role to play in teaching everyone in their organizations how to spot future trends, work effectively across functions, spawn promising new ideas, innovate, be flexible, know when to exit existing businesses, and much more. Winning organizations are constantly implementing smart change—not just change for change's sake.

Leaders can and must be developed at all levels of the organization for it to thrive. While all the essays in this book deal with leadership challenges, I have organized them into sections that focus on the different issues leaders confront:

Leadership DNA: What Separates a Leader from Everyone Else?
Leaders aren't born, but they share unique traits that separate them from everyone else.
Leadership Comes in All Shapes and Styles
Leaders can be found in places as diverse as the US Marine Corps, college marching bands, and even your own family.
Leadership Is Not a Solo Flight
Leaders understand that everyone is a stakeholder—employees, customers, the board of directors, shareholders, and suppliers.

Preface

Leaders Don't Grow on Trees

Leaders focus on cultivating future leaders instead of obsessing about short-term profits and their own immediate success.

Why Branding and Marketing Matter

Leaders value branding and marketing as critical components of an organization's success; they do not consider them expenses to be cut on a whim.

Leaders Lead, Bosses Boss

Leaders know the difference between leading and bossing; they also know when to say "when."

In baseball, extra innings often mean stretching out your bullpen and using bench players. In business it's called "bandwidth." In either case, you can't rely on your stars alone to always pull you through—everyone on the team has to be prepared to perform. I am one of those people who believe that pressure is almost always self-inflicted. In extra innings, every play and every at bat brings pressure. The winners are those who perform well under pressure and who welcome the challenge. It's no different in business.

"Never go through life saying I should have but didn't."
　　　—*My father's advice when I joined the navy after*
　　　graduating from college during the Vietnam War

SECTION I

Leadership DNA:
What Separates a Leader
from Everyone Else?

"Exemplary leaders go first."
—*James M. Kouzes and Barry Z. Posner*

1.
Leadership Begins
with Trust

Scandals are an unfortunate part of life. At the time I was putting this book together, the scandals du jour included the IRS allegedly targeting conservative groups, government eavesdropping on Associated Press reporters, and the Benghazi embassy tragedy. If we go back a few years, you'll no doubt remember the following:

- New York Governor Eliot Spitzer resigned after first denying and then admitting to having patronized a high-priced prostitution ring.

- AIG, after receiving an $85 billion bailout from the federal government, was discovered sending its top performers to a lavish spa weekend. Approximately 24 hours later the Federal Reserve provided AIG with an additional $37 billion.

- Presidential aspirant and former US Senator John Edwards denied and later admitted to an extramarital affair while his wife battled breast cancer.

- The CEO of Merrill Lynch spent more than $1 million renovating his personal office while the company hemorrhaged.

- Bernie Madoff's $60 billion-plus Ponzi scheme was the largest investor fraud committed by a single person.

- The IRS was accused of targeting conservative groups as they applied for 501(c)3 nonprofit status. The terms used to single out applications were keywords like "conservative," "Tea Party," and others.

It should come as no surprise then that American workers have lost trust in their leaders. In fact, many feel betrayed. True leaders are not promiscuous with the truth.

Why is it so important that employee trust be restored? When you think about it, the answers are pretty clear. Trust

- unleashes higher performance,

- reduces operational costs,

- eliminates needless litigation,

- retains the most productive workers,

- perpetuates the most desirable aspects of a company's culture,

- builds an esprit de corps, and

- sustains financial success, especially in times of unprecedented, complex change.

So, how do you restore employee trust after scandal has ripped at the fabric of so many once-prized organizations and institutions? As both a practitioner and student of leadership for more than three decades, I offer the following seven remedies:

1. Hire CEOs on the basis of their moral fiber as a starter. Webster defines trust as "reliance on the integrity, strength and ability" of a person.

2. Ensure the board of directors more closely monitors and objectively evaluates the CEO's behavior as well as performance on the job and off.

3. Practice former President Ronald Reagan's signature phrase from the Russian proverb—*Dovorey no provorey*—"Trust, but verify."[1] We have all seen too many examples where boards abdicated their governance roles and, as such, their roles as corporate watchdogs.

4. Realign compensation programs so that the wide gulf between executives and rank-and-file workers is narrowed significantly.

5. Institute a practice that CEOs must be transparent, authentic leaders who possess the skills to convince employees they are genuinely valued as partners in the enterprise. CEOs can accomplish this goal by consistent actions that over time demonstrate they place employees first. The chairman emeritus of the Herman Miller Company gracefully and poignantly once said, "Leadership is much more than a set of things to do: it is an art, a belief, a condition of the heart."[2]

6. Have no hidden agenda, share information as fully and as broadly as you can, and never forget that there is no such thing as a private conversation. In other words, give the same information to each of your constituencies.

7. CEOs are mortal beings who make mistakes. When you do, own up to it and let others know.

Remember, trust is essential to organizational success. It is what makes the team go round. Robert Eckert, former chairman and CEO of Mattel, believes, "As you go to work, your top responsibility should be to build trust."[3]

2.

Leaders Learn from Adversity

Savvy interviewers have learned to ask promising job candidates the question, "What has been the biggest failure you've experienced or the most difficult challenge that you've faced thus far in life?" For most of us, the rationale behind the question is the search to learn how the person rebounded from his or her adversity.

Two of my favorite Biblical quotes are Philippians 4:12–13 and Proverbs 24:10. The former reads, "I know how to be brought low, and I know how to abound. In any and every circumstance, I have learned the secret of facing plenty and hunger, abundance and need. I can do all things through him who strengthens me."[1] The latter reads, "If you faint in the day of adversity, your strength is small."[2]

Leadership Requires Extra Innings

I have long believed that great leaders have had to overcome adversity in one form or another. How else can one explain why some leaders have an innate ability to inspire a workforce to reach new heights, summoning their best work, their indefatigable spirit, and complete trust while others fail so miserably? It's not how much formal education they received, their rearing, or any number of other factors. Great leaders have an inner strength and confidence in themselves that most likely was developed as they failed miserably at something earlier in life but developed a resolve not to stay down. They may have been born with a malady they had to overcome, or they faced an atrocity or even death. Several examples are particularly worth noting:

- Paul Orfalea, Kinko's founder and author of *Copy This!* was a hyperactive dyslexic.

- The late Bill Walsh, the San Francisco 49ers coach and general manager, was blackballed earlier by Cleveland Bengals coach Paul Brown, nearly ending Walsh's career in the NFL.

- Senator John McCain was imprisoned and frequently tortured in the "Hanoi Hilton" prison in North Vietnam.

- Renowned architect Frank Gehry had to overcome anti-Semitic abuse early in life.

- Marlee Matlin, a profoundly deaf actress, won an Academy Award.

- The late Senator Daniel Inouye, a Japanese American and World War II hero, was severely wounded in combat, losing his hand.

- Paige Vickery overcame Tourette's syndrome to become a highly successful classical musician and conductor.

Management guru Warren Bennis has labeled this ability to overcome severe challenges as "adaptive capacity…an almost magical ability to transcend adversity, with all its attendant stresses, and to emerge stronger than before."[3] He says it is composed of two primary qualities: the ability to grasp context and hardiness.

I had the pleasure of speaking with General Tony Zinni in San Francisco. Zinni, the highly decorated retired US Marine, former CENTCOM commander in chief, diplomat, presidential adviser, and confidant to several corporate CEOs, wrote *Leading the Charge: Leadership Lessons from the Battlefield to the Boardroom.*

It is Zinni's belief that "people are desperate for leadership they can trust and depend on." He says, "The new leaders must be able to operate at a blisteringly fast pace and be quick to harness ever-evolving technologies."[4] If Zinni and others are correct in these assessments that a major reordering of the world is occurring and that we are experiencing a "shakeup" like no other, it becomes rather clear that we need leaders who have been shaped by adversity—leaders who have the ability and toughness to place things in proper perspective, a perseverance to get up, be stronger than before, and succeed.

It might be well for us all to heed the African proverb: "Smooth seas do not make skillful sailors."[5]

3.
Leaders Have Guts

I was listening to newspaper columnists and former White House press secretaries debate the positions of national leaders on ABC's *This Week* and was reminded once again of a very important quality that makes for effective leadership: guts.

Today's political climate has been accurately described as ugly. All sides on many issues often refuse to consider other points of view or to compromise for the greater good, and too many leaders on all sides of the spectrum seem fearful of making the tough decisions for fear of alienating their base of support.

It's a shame our political leaders don't heed the wisdom attributed to management guru Peter Drucker that "wherever you see a successful business, someone has made a courageous decision."[1] Fortunately, we still witness among us courageous actions taken by true leaders who understand what is needed for making the tough decisions. Following are a few examples.

Former Secretary of Defense Robert Gates, appointed to his position by President George W. Bush, was wisely retained by President Barack Obama. Gates made a difficult but correct decision to recommend that Gen. Stanley McChrystal be relieved of his position as the top US commander in Afghanistan. Though he was a highly decorated and distinguished flag officer, McChrystal neglected to follow counsel offered by retired Marine Gen. James Jones, then national security adviser, to give his candid recommendations to the president in private. Senate Armed Services Committee members Sens. Lindsey Graham (R-SC) and John McCain (R-AZ) quickly backed Gates's recommendation and Obama's decision to relieve McChrystal.

Columbia University President Lee Bollinger made what he knew was going to be a controversial decision by inviting Iranian President Mahmoud Ahmadinejad to speak at Columbia's New York campus. A First Amendment scholar, Bollinger was severely criticized for the invitation and for his own remarks that day, but we learned much more about the Iranian leader as a result of Bollinger's courageous decision to invite him to speak.

Factory owner Aaron Feuerstein's decision to continue to pay his employees after his textile factory in Lawrence, Massachusetts, burned to the ground will long stand as one of the most courageous and thoughtful acts ever taken by a business leader. He truly embodies what reporter Rebecca Leung referred to as the "Mensch of Malden Mills."[2]

While at GE, Jack Welch was legendary for jettisoning those General Electric businesses that, while highly profitable, were unlikely to ever be the best in their industries. It takes courage to commit to excellence and then ensure that anything less isn't worth doing. Welch fostered a corporate culture of being fast, agile, and lean and thinking like a small company.

Joe Torre, the former Yankees skipper, surprised most everyone in 1996 by brilliantly managing the pinstripers to capture the World Series while courageously keeping the front office at bay. He is revered for speaking out about his abusive father and establishing his Safe At Home Foundation for prevention of domestic violence.

There are many leadership qualities worth emulating. In the sports world, the expression "no pain, no gain" is heard every day. In the military, those defending our country are taught "no guts, no glory." Having played varsity sports in high school and college, and also having been a Navy officer, I have found that playing it safe seldom gets the strategic win.

Perhaps Albert Einstein said it best: "Great spirits have always encountered violent opposition from mediocre minds. The mediocre mind is incapable of understanding the man who refuses to bow blindly to conventional prejudices and chooses instead to express his opinions courageously and honestly."[3]

4.
Leaders Have Passion

Whenever there's an election, we hear a lot about the qualities of leadership and what inspires an individual to believe in and follow another. One of the words often bandied about (and for good reason) is "passion."

Effective leaders understand that passion is not only desirable but also required. In fact, few qualities of leadership are more important. That's because we the people want to know that our leaders—in government, business, places of worship, sports, and elsewhere—fervently ascribe to what they are saying. We want to know that our leaders' views will not be easily swayed or mysteriously vanish when times get tough. Above all, we want to believe that the actions of those in leadership are motivated by a strong sense of purpose and by values they are passionate about.

But where does passion come from? What is the alchemy by which it is brewed? For some, passion is rooted in life experiences. History is filled with stories of individuals who through life's journey unearth a passion that had otherwise been dormant. From the politician who is exposed to the plight of those less fortunate for the first time, to the college professor who taps into a treasure buried deep inside his or her student, passion can spring from life's understanding and awakening. Once it does, nothing is ever the same again.

Passion can also be instilled in very young children, as it is modeled by parents and discussed at the family dinner table alongside other important lessons like the value of hard work and not giving up in the face of adversity. It is then that parents do their best parenting. It is from these moments that their children begin to see the splendor of finding what drives them—something they care deeply about and that they want to share with others in a compelling and memorable way. It is from such sparks that tomorrow's leaders are often born.

We see passion all around us every day: teachers who care, nurses who go the extra mile, pastors who reach out, and neighbors who want to make their community a better place to live. Sadly, we see misguided passion as well. Graveyards are full of young men and women who were passionate in their cause but whose poorly placed obsessions led to jealousy, hate, bitterness, or worse—suffering, war, and social injustice. The lesson from such tragedies is clear: Passion without virtue to guide it is meaningless.

In this important time, it is the role of all of us to instill passion in our young. Show them the beauty of caring deeply about an idea, a goal, or a mission and then motivating others to care deeply as well. Real leaders know how to express their own passions and tap into the wants, hopes, and dreams of those around them.

Those leaders who have touched our lives and made indelible impressions have had the ability to do just that, not merely through words but through countless unselfish acts where their passion has been obvious for all to see. They are the best our society has to offer and the embodiment of Oliver Wendell Holmes's challenge that "life is action and passion; therefore, it is required of a man that he should share the passion and action of the time, at peril of being judged not to have lived."[1]

5.
Leaders Are Accountable

Though scandal is hardly new in business, government, or college athletics, the recent past has been particularly difficult to fathom in terms of scale and utter disregard for rules and standards.

Not unlike Paris Hilton and Lindsay Lohan, our supposedly grown-up leaders have become repeat offenders, unable to learn the lessons of the past and loath to believe that what happened to Bernie Madoff, Lehman Brothers, and Worldcom could also happen to them.

Consider the following events that occurred in just a two-year period:

- Though Rupert Murdoch claims to have known nothing of the phone hacking activities of his newspaper *News of the World*, the scandal has forever damaged his once sterling reputation.

Lesson: Know what's going on in your organization at every level.

• Arnold Schwarzenegger's previously unknown child by a past lover, Anthony Weiner's sexting fiasco, Eric Massa's tickle fights with pages, and the very sad John Edwards saga have shown ethics breaches that have caused the public to wonder if these "leaders" have misunderstood the meaning of the phrase "political party." We have seen them all face deep, personal consequences for their abuses. *Lesson:* Be accountable for actions that compromise your integrity to lead.

• The British Petroleum Deepwater Horizon oil spill has turned out to be a catastrophe that could have been avoided simply by following basic safety measures and paying attention to test results. BP's leaders compounded the damage of the spill by making callous statements to victims and denying the enormity of the catastrophe. *Lesson:* Don't cut corners where it counts.

• Former Congressman Tom DeLay (R-TX) has been in and out of trouble for years, suspected of fraud and moving campaign money illegally. He was convicted (2010), sentenced and later his conviction was overturned by an appeals court and the government may appeal. With a huge cloud over his head and facing a very tough reelection bid, he resigned his seat in the House of Representatives. *Lesson:* Don't put yourself in compromising situations.

- Ironically, the organization involved in one of the biggest ethics scandals of 2010, Wikileaks, could turn out to be a deterring force for unethical behavior in the future. Governments are finding it hard to prosecute the organization, whose founders and board remain anonymous, except for spokesman Julian Assange, because of free-speech protection.

  Lesson: Know your ethical boundaries.

- Since 2011 the NCAA has been investigating the University of Miami football program, including allegations of an imprisoned ex-Hurricanes booster. If substantiated, it will make the sanctions imposed for rules violations committed by Ohio State, USC, North Carolina, and others look mild by comparison. However, now the University of Miami asks for the "corrupted" NCAA investigation to end and has informed the organization's governing body "that it will stipulate to any properly corroborated allegations against the Hurricanes if the case is brought to a swift end and without any further penalties."[1]

  Lesson: Take control and reform, reform, reform.

One positive outgrowth of all of this shameful behavior is that the leadership community appears to be taking note. Corporations have begun implementing ethics retraining or hotlines that employees can use to anonymously report dangerous practices. A few CEOs at major companies are even beginning to make modest sacrifices in the form of personal pay cuts.

After Standard & Poor's downgraded the nation's credit status, business leaders began to see the need to go public with statements that indicate a turn in thinking. Warren Buffett famously called for lawmakers to "stop coddling the super rich" and increase the tax rate for millionaires and billionaires.[2]

Starbucks' CEO Howard Schultz announced he would withhold political contributions until lawmakers stop bickering and come up with a plan for debt and runaway spending. These kinds of measures are rapidly winning support.

Leaders need to demand accountability—and be held accountable for breaking the rules and wrecking the system on which everyone depends.

6.
Leaders Lead by Example

Especially during the holiday season, our thoughts naturally turn to people who are truly making a difference in the world. A few that come to mind include one current and two former professional athletes I believe are especially notable: David Robinson, Charles Woodson, and Dikembe Mutombo.

Each of these men is, or was, a giant in his respective "business." Robinson, the well-known US Naval Academy graduate, excelled as a student in Annapolis, led the midshipmen to three consecutive NCAA tournaments, and was named the Sporting News College Player of the Year in 1987. After fulfilling his commitment as a naval officer, "The Admiral," as he was often called, joined the National Basketball Association and subsequently won numerous individual and team awards, including Rookie of the Year, two NBA championships with the San Antonio Spurs, and two Olympic Gold Medals. He was inducted into the Naismith Memorial Basketball Hall of Fame in 2009.

Woodson, the former University of Michigan All-American and Heisman Trophy–winning cornerback, is enjoying a distinguished National Football League career. He is also the only NCAA Division I-A football player to win college football's most prestigious award as a defensive player.

Mutombo, a native of Zaire (now the Democratic Republic of the Congo) and a Georgetown University graduate who played for John Thompson's Hoyas basketball team, once blocked 12 shots in a single game. "Deke" went on to become one of the NBA's most prolific shot blockers in his 16-year career and earned four Defensive Player of the Year awards.

That these three men were successful in their chosen professions is an understatement. But it is what they thought about and did during and after their sports careers that is both remarkable and memorable.

In 2001, David Robinson and his wife, Valerie, founded the Carver Academy in San Antonio, Texas, with their $5 million gift (when I last checked a few years ago, they had given more than $11 million to the Carver Complex and other San Antonio inner-city programs). The school provides prekindergarten through sixth-grade students an education of excellence, regardless of race, creed, or financial status. Carver Academy inspires students to exemplify leadership, discipline, and initiative—the characteristics Robinson embodied at "the boat school" and throughout his NBA career.

Now an Oakland Raider, NFL All Pro Charles Woodson donated $2 million to the University of Michigan's C.S. Mott Children's Hospital and Women's Hospital. Woodson's gift will be earmarked for pediatric research. Woodson's devotion to research efforts designed to finding cures for pediatric cancer, heart disease, kidney disorders, and autism speaks volumes for this publicity-shy Wolverine.

Mutombo, founder of a state-of-the-art hospital and medical research facility in Kinshasa (Congo), is remarkable for his commitment to humanity. In the Congo, more than 500,000 children die each year before they reach age 5, most from preventable causes. Among other services, his hospital will train several hundred clinicians and improve treatment of HIV/AIDS patients.

The British historian Thomas Macaulay once wrote: "The measure of a man's real character is what he would do if he knew he would never be found out."[1] David Robinson, Charles Woodson, and Dikembe Mutombo are three media-reticent, reserved men who share a common bond: to make the world a much better place for the less fortunate and to focus the spotlight on the people being helped, rather than on themselves.

I have always believed that one person's actions can make a positive difference in the lives of others. Most of us do not have the star power of a David Robinson, Charles Woodson, or Dikembe Mutombo, but all three of them would no doubt agree that, no matter who you are, helping those in need has a rippling effect.

7.
Leaders Love to Teach:
Enlarging the Playing Field

A cross the globe, leaders struggle with a multitude of crises, including major fiscal challenges, rising acts of terrorism, rapidly changing technologies, the environment, and much more. In the United States, partisanship and rancor, rather than compromise and consensus, rule the day from Sacramento to Washington, DC. The absence of effective leadership is unfortunately not limited to the halls of Congress but continues to plague both Wall Street financiers and C-suite executives. One has to ask why leaders are unwilling or unable to act with a greater sense of urgency in addressing the myriad challenges facing their organizations.

In his 2008 best seller, *A Sense of Urgency*, noted change expert John Kotter posits that "as we transition to a world where change is continuous—not episodic—urgency must become a core, sustained capability."[1] A major focus of our attention should be to take immediate steps to encourage more senior leaders to not only act with this sense of urgency but also to ensure a sustainable future by becoming teachers and mentors of younger talent within their own companies.

History has taught us that crises such as those we're facing today often produce successful leaders—that leaders are made, not born. In *Crucibles of Leadership*, management guru Warren Bennis and his colleague Robert Thomas suggest that the ability to overcome adversity is one of the most reliable predictors of leadership success. In *Where Have All the Leaders Gone?* Lee Iacocca points out that we need mentors, those who can teach us how to lead.

The central challenge we face is finding leaders who can tackle the urgent problems of today while teaching and developing future leaders as they go. As acclaimed management experts Noel Tichy and Eli Cohen have written in *The Leadership Engine*: "The job of the leader has not changed. Enhancing the value of assets and sustaining growth are still the ultimate goals. This is accomplished by developing others to be leaders at every level and getting them aligned and energized."[2]

Two practical, concrete action steps must be taken for this to occur. First, businesses and institutions must commit to becoming "teaching" organizations, ones where a conscious pledge is made to teach managers how to become leaders. The need for such resolute commitment is both obvious and practical: presidents, CEOs, and members of the executive team who take the time to teach, mentor, and guide their lieutenants experience more success in driving operating performance.

Retention of key personnel is heightened and costs are lessened in those organizations that effectively leverage the talent of their staffs. And, as experience has shown, executives who teach and mentor become stronger leaders.

In my judgment, the best organizations to work for are those who consciously and genuinely invest in their employees' futures, including leadership development. Farsighted leaders understand the sheer power of lifelong learning—for these programs to realize their full potential, several elements must be constant, some of which are:

- Company leaders, especially C-suite executives, must not simply attend leadership training modules, they need to lead them often and be active participants

- These same leaders need to realize that they must be accessible by openly sharing both their successes and failures—and how they grew as a result of those experiences

- Leaders must ensure that employee development—specifically leadership development—is practical and composed of actual problems, integrated in all relevant company management practices, allows for honest feedback, and that participants will be held accountable for their performance in the program

- The CEO must be the number one champion and protector of the organizational culture while at the same time being the chief architect and voice of how the organization must change to achieve greater success

8.
Leaders Have Vision

Hardly a day goes by without some academic, financial pundit, or media personality decrying the fact that neither Congress nor the White House seems to have a clear vision for solving the nation's ills.

To listen to them, you would think it's a rather simple exercise to craft a cohesive vision. It is not. If you don't believe me, just ask most any chief executive officer who has been at the helm of a company for more than a few years.

To paraphrase what Jim Collins and Jerry Porras opined in their seminal 1996 *Harvard Business Review* article "Building Your Company's Vision," the degree of difficulty in crafting a bold vision is heightened by the need to understand what should be changed in an organization and what must not.

Crafting a vision that simultaneously lifts people up and generates decisive execution would go a long way toward resolving the nation's challenges. However, creating a vision requires making choices and having the will to take risks, especially in today's politically polarized environment.

The most important purpose of a vision is to set forth a discernible direction and a commitment to that direction. On the national front, it is developed principally for the purpose of achieving the country's success—not just to win an election. In the Senate, Minority Leader Mitch McConnell (R-KY) seemed determined to do everything he could to ensure that Barack Obama was a one-term president, while Majority Leader Harry Reid (D-NV) seemed equally determined to frustrate the GOP at every turn.

While their actions often support their personal or political views, they do little to address real problems. An effective vision is not campaign rhetoric; nor does it use emotional tactics. It provides a clear blueprint of where a president intends to take us and then engages us with the possibilities. It is specific, not inclusive, easily understood, straightforward, and, yes, bold.

That is why staffers or assistants should never craft a vision statement. The person who intends to articulate and live by it must exercise the discipline to write the first drafts so the result genuinely and accurately reflects his or her beliefs.

One doesn't need special powers to realize we live in turbulent, uncertain, and dangerous times, internationally and domestically. Such circumstances require highly credible and convincing visions. Americans will follow a leader who not only has an inspirational vision but who also articulates it well, integrates it, and fully commits to its success.

In my book *Real Leaders Don't Boss*, I describe effective leaders from all walks of life, many of whom I've known personally. I firmly believe that we suffer less from a scarcity of real leaders in America than we do from apathy and an inexplicable willingness to accept less than what we want from our leaders, elected or appointed.

Our political leaders are all rather good at telling convincing narratives, which can ultimately bring a vision to life. But what we really need from all our leaders—political and otherwise— is less time on peripheral issues and more focus on outlining visions for the future.

In his *New York Times* best seller *Strategic Vision*, Zbigniew Brzezinski provides a desperately needed wake-up call to America's political and business leaders as the world's center of gravity shifts from the West to the East. At the top of his list is a call for resolving our domestic problems—until we do, our international opportunities and options will be seriously curtailed.

9.
The Top 10 Traits of Real Leaders

A fter returning from visiting Mt. Vernon and a number of other historical sites on the East Coast, my thoughts turned to Independence Day and leadership crucibles.

In my early career, I was fortunate to know and interact with leaders who inspired me and became an influence for the rest of my life. Though things have changed a lot since I was young, one thing is still true: leaders must inspire their people in the workplace if they are to succeed.

Ken Blanchard, author and management guru, once remarked: "In the past a leader was a boss. Today's leaders must be partners with their people; they no longer can lead based on positional power."[1]

Successful leaders of today must cultivate a different set of traits than leaders of the past. In today's workplace, intimidation and bullying are no longer tolerated as a management style, and are considered detrimental to long-term productivity and the well-being of the organization.

The following is a list of 10 traits that are important for successful leadership:

1. *A genuine love of ideas and people.* This includes those that may be disagreeable to some of us. One must be able to look beyond the ideas a person expresses or behavior he or she exhibits in the moment to grasp the whole person.

2. *Trustworthiness.* Good leaders do what they say they will do and do not lie.

3. *A passion to succeed by doing what is right.* A leader must set high standards and teach and mentor others to succeed.

4. *Culture consciousness.* A leader understands that the workplace culture sets the context from which everything evolves. He or she must examine how employees interact and cultivate a positive environment.

5. *A sense of humor.* The ability to use humor constructively and positively sets others at ease in your presence.

6. *A drive to make the world a better place.* A leader can help people see purpose in their jobs beyond their day-to-day duties.

7. *Humility.* It is important to be able to effortlessly and genuinely give credit to others.

8. *The ability to speak in a clear, respectful, down-to-earth manner.* This also puts people at ease. Eliminating confusion about the organization's mission promotes productivity by preventing delays.

9. *An engaging personality.* A successful leader is someone who others want to be around.

10. *A knack for being both adaptive and enduring.* Leaders are flexible enough to be able to shift gears as circumstances demand while still maintaining long-term goals.

Cultivating these traits produces confident, effective leadership better able to manage a workforce. It also produces a more contented, more committed employee base willing to work hard to promote the organization's goals. As a leader, you may or may not possess every one of these characteristics, but learning to improve in these traits will make you a more effective leader, a more confident person, and will most likely make your job easier and more enjoyable.

True leaders realize, as did our Founding Fathers, that inspired leadership is about moral responsibility and accountability and involves taking their staffs to places they probably wouldn't go on their own. They also ensure their people are heard, involved, and trained to be more innovative in moving the company forward.

Leadership comes from the top, but people at every level of the organization are engaged. As a result, these inspiring leaders advance their organizations to new heights every day.

10.
All Leaders Should Know
How to Write

How many leaders of major organizations write their own web page greeting, presentations, annual report message to shareholders, or letters to the editor? According to Noel Tichy, some "90% of CEOs have someone else" write for them. [1]

The growing reliance on ghostwriters to craft a myriad of official communiqués, e-mail messages, blogs, or correspondence is an increasingly troubling practice in many organizations. Much more often than we realize, executives task their in-house public relations team, human resources staff, legal department, or external consultants to draft an important epistle. If integrity, transparency, and authenticity are prized leadership qualities sought by governing boards in their quest for new leaders (and I believe they must be), then it follows that employees, customers, suppliers, and other key stakeholders should reasonably expect that the organization's top tier of leaders write the first draft of their most important messages. Subsequent reviews of executives' drafts by the previously mentioned specialists are often necessary and appropriate but they cannot take the place of original thinking. Genuine executive communications might well help reverse the disturbing fact that "two out of every five new CEOs fail in their first 18 months."[2]

While some notable CEOs have written their own blogs (for example, Jonathan Swartz while at Sun Microsystems and John Chambers of Cisco), you may remember the *Wall Street Journal's* reporting of the bizarre example of misguided CEO behavior when Whole Foods CEO John Mackey used a pseudonym (an anagram of his wife's first name) in a blog for seven years in an attempt to influence customers' views and stock prices. While the SEC ruled it was not unlawful, it was, nonetheless, poor judgment. B. L. Ochman reported that a Times of London international poll of 750 bloggers revealed that "only two out of ten senior business executives actually write their own blog posts."[3] On the other hand, Warren Buffett and Jeff Bezos are well known for personally writing their own very stimulating "Annual Report" letters to shareholders.

In his acclaimed work *American Sphinx: The Character of Thomas Jefferson*, Joseph Ellis writes: "The art of making decisions was synonymous with the art of drafting and revising texts."[4] According to Harold Holzer, author of *Lincoln President-Elect*, despite facing arguably the biggest challenge of a young republic when he took office, Abraham Lincoln did not employ a speechwriter. Both leaders invited their cabinets to suggest ideas for possible inclusion in the drafts of their speeches and both shared drafts of what they had written, but the first drafts were theirs.

Following are four important reasons why leaders of any major business—a for-profit company, a city, a university, or a civic organization—should commit to recapture this lost art:

1. CEOs are hired to formulate and chart the most strategic direction for their organizations. They are expected to allocate the required time to accomplish this. While sage counsel is critical, these responsibilities simply should not be outsourced or delegated. The intellectual rigor and reflection required should be that of the CEO and the executive team. Translating time spent on these important activities into writing is a crucial skill that sharpens one's focus, leading to less confusion and rework, increased trust and inspired followership, and, most importantly, improved outcomes.

2. We expect our leaders to establish a compelling vision, adhere to the organization's mission, strengthen the corporate culture, and set and effectively communicate the direction for achieving results. Writing forces leaders to be clear, concise, and cogent for the required followership. Former Secretary of State and Chairman of the Joint Chiefs of Staff Army General Colin Powell said: "Successful leaders know how to define their mission and convey it to their subordinates...."[5]

3. After observing and interacting with the CEO (who is hopefully an enviable role model), executive team members

must pass on lessons learned to junior staff. As anyone who has taught leadership can attest, one learns the most about how to become a leader through experience—not by being in the classroom listening to a faculty member or analyzing a case study. By writing one's thoughts out first, then sharing them with others, inviting feedback, and discussing alternative ideas, the leaders' writing improves but so, too, do subordinates' leadership skills. Mid-level and junior leaders learn by writing action plans and position statements that hone their ability to communicate more effectively.

4. CEOs should expect their executives to be teachers because it serves to keep the organization's top leaders well informed and aware of shifting markets and competitive terrain. In a university setting, for example, administrators who typically have little contact with students can give a guest lecture or teach a class in their area of expertise. Regular engagement with students helps them become and remain sound leaders as they have to read more widely, develop a demanding course syllabus, pen learning objectives, give lectures, and, most importantly, communicate effectively on relevant topics. Former Allied Signal and Honeywell CEO Larry Bossidy, who rarely expected his staff to do his writing, commented that "good people come to companies and stay because they believe they have a chance to expand their capabilities and fulfill their destiny. You have an obligation to help them."[6]

I can think of no easier way for CEOs to lose legitimacy than if their vision is unclear or unconvincing. CEOs who write the first drafts of their major messages are much more likely to rally stakeholders in ways no speechwriter can imitate.

*"At the end of the day you bet on people,
not on strategies."*

— *Larry Bossidy*

SECTION II

Leadership Comes in All
Shapes and Styles

11.
Leader or Boss?

Who among us hasn't had a bad boss? And yet, who has not been influenced by a leader who exhibited inspirational qualities like focus, strategic know-how, and an instinct for grasping what is important and when? Having one or the other as an influence can determine the atmosphere of a company and how successfully it will run.

A 2010 research report by the Conference Board on Americans' job satisfaction confirms what was obvious to most of us already: there is tremendous discontent in today's workplace that stifles innovation and creativity at a time when we need it the most.

Much of this responsibility weighs on the shoulders of those in leadership positions—those who have the say-so as to what kind of atmosphere prevails. But what are the qualities that set good leaders apart?

During much of my working life, I've reported to or consulted with CEOs or chairmen of the board. This opportunity to see a variety of chief executives in action practically everywhere has often been very good—and sometimes horrendous.

I have dealt with bosses who were philanderers, racists, bullies, and egomaniacs with anger-management problems. Many were intellectually bright, but their behaviors undermined the success their organizations could have achieved under real leadership.

My personal experience with both types of individuals has enabled me to create a mosaic of what I believe differentiates one who leads from one who merely supervises:

- A leader focuses on long-term results and positions the organization for ongoing success; a boss is too concerned about the next quarter's bottom line to have a big-picture perspective.

- A leader is a champion for his or her employees. A boss tends to see his or her employees as a means to an end.

- A leader connects directly with all stakeholders, including employees. He or she takes the time to listen and respond in a thoughtful and humble manner that celebrates people. A boss, on the other hand, often pays lip service to direct reports and is more focused on his or her own well-being. Bosses generally disregard employees who are not direct reports.

- A leader shows congeniality and respect to everyone

regardless of his or her position in the organization. The boss may seek to be pleasant and charming to executives but is indifferent or even demeaning toward others. The saying "smiles up the organization and frowns down the organization" captures the point well.

- A leader will prohibit his managers from being demeaning, disrespectful, or verbally abusive to others. A boss often turns his back on such behavior and may exhibit it himself.

- Leaders recognize that all employees, including themselves, have a right to a balanced life. A boss tends to micromanage and overload his or her team with tasks that have impossible due dates.

- A leader will seek to remove obstacles for his employees and provide the necessary resources and expedite processes, making it easier for others to accomplish their jobs, while a boss may throw roadblocks in front of employees in ways that cause rework and unnecessary frustration.

The definition of a leader should apply to any person in a decision-making capacity, formal or informal, who advances the strategic goals of the business, who contributes mightily to institutional performance, and who treats people fairly, honestly, and compassionately.

Those who would strive to be defined in this way should also remember the following seven keys to effective leadership:

1. Commit to driving fear out of your organization with honest communication and with no tolerance regarding unprofessional behavior.

2. Discipline or weed out those who undermine performance and morale.

3. Strengthen corporate culture with discipline and compassion.

4. Believe in and build up your team. Take an interest in them as human beings and encourage creative, morale-building behaviors and activities.

5. Give clear assignments, and then get out of the way. Let others have the chance to execute successfully.

6. Be accessible and listen.

7. Display high integrity and humility in everything you do.

Though perfect execution of all of these qualities will have its challenges, the logic behind them is basic: it comes down to treating people right and doing what's right not for yourself, but for others and for the company as a whole.

Perhaps the idea is most succinctly put by Scott Monty, social media head at Ford Motor Co., who described his boss Alan Mulally as "the real deal," a leader who inspires by "simply being a decent human being."[1]

12.
Leadership the Marines Way

When President Obama decided to send 21,000 additional US military personnel to Afghanistan hoping to eliminate insurgent strongholds, the first US servicemen and women to arrive were approximately 10,000 Marines. As I read about this, I was reminded of my visit to the 135-acre National Museum of the Marine Corps in Quantico, Virginia.

Museum visitors are greeted upon entering by several quotations that adorn the walls. As a student of leadership, I was struck by one common thread in the following testimonials: there are no quotes written by Marines.

"At Iwo Jima, uncommon valor was a common virtue."

—Fleet Admiral Chester Nimitz, US Navy

"The safest place in Korea was right behind a platoon of Marines. Lord, how they could fight."

—Major General Frank E. Lowe, US Army

"I never think of a Marine but what I think of a man who wants to do more, not less; a man you have to hold back, not shove."

—President Lyndon B. Johnson

"They have tradition; the U.S. Marines bear upon their shoulders the nation's past and the nation's hope for the future."

—Hanson W. Baldwin, *The New York Times*

The leadership qualities that American presidents so often consider when sending America's military, especially Marines, "in harm's way" are remarkably similar to leadership crucibles that high-performance organizations can adapt. Refined over 200 years of severe tests of bravery and sacrifice, here are six of the most important:

1. Consistently delivering results: an unshakable "can do" attitude and relentless passion to exceed the goal

2. Never quitting, living out the motto "lead, follow, or get out of the way"

3. An enduring service culture characterized by a fiercely proud tradition, honor, discipline, humility, and a promise to never leave anyone behind

4. Always ready: a remarkable adaptive and persevering ability, a trained flexibility to overcome any obstacle—to do more with fewer resources than others

5. Leadership that is consistently and transparently held to a higher standard than the rest of the organization, to always "carry the torch" and be paragons of inspiration to their troops

6. Unafraid of admitting shortcomings and always committed to make it right

As Howard Engel referred to them, the "battlefields of the marketplace" also call upon business leaders to be adaptive, operate frugally, be courageous, and inspire employees.[1] In his book *On Becoming a Leader,* Warren Bennis cites numerous examples of the leader's need to conceive and sell his or her vision.

The Marines' talent engine is one worth emulating. They assign their best to recruiting for a fixed period of time. How many businesses can say the same about their human resources departments?

The Corps leadership pool is another enviable model. The adage "Those who can't do, teach" doesn't apply as all Marines are expected to teach. Values are instilled, pride is amplified, and storytelling is elevated to an art form so tough decisions can be made.

Courage is an expectation that permeates the Marine Corps. It is also a requirement for success in the workplace. Taking the business into unchartered waters is not for the meek. Neither is competing with fierce, stronger brands or launching new products in a crowded market.

Is it any wonder that the University of Pennsylvania's prestigious Wharton School has taken its students to Quantico to listen, observe, and learn from Marines to integrate their leadership lessons into the university's management curriculum?

13.
Performing Arts:
An Overlooked Leadership Lab

California Lutheran University has grown substantially in academic stature, diversity, physical environment, and enrollment since it was founded in 1959. Early Conejo Valley pioneers, including Richard Pederson (who donated the land for the new college), would marvel at the myriad ways Cal Lutheran has blossomed into the fine institution it is today.

Despite the phenomenal growth, one major facility is still noticeably lacking on the CLU campus—a center to house the performing arts.

Some of my CLU friends and former colleagues have made a passionate and persuasive case that the university would be better served through a new science center, additional scholarships, an enhanced study-abroad program, or an alumni house. All of these are worthwhile endeavors and all have merit. But if you look at other campuses around CLU as well as nationwide, to become a full-fledged university that fulfills the needs of all its constituencies, a performing arts complex is essential.

The promise of a center for the performing arts offers innumerable benefits to future students, faculty, local families and other residents, and CLU alumni. It also just happens to be a major magnet for prospective donors. In other words, it makes good business sense.

The theater arts and music departments at Cal Lutheran have long been recognized for their high quality and ability to graduate leaders in the creative arts. But they are severely handicapped by being forced to perform in buildings that were not designed for such purposes. To the departments' joint credit, they have weathered this limitation with enormous success as witnessed by the fact that productions of the theater arts department have been selected numerous times to perform at the prestigious Region VIII Kennedy Center's American College of Theatre Festival, and the choir has performed at New York's Lincoln Center and in England, Italy, Norway, and Sweden.

A performing arts center at CLU would not only showcase these tremendous programs but would also provide a new bridge to further connect the university to future students and the community in the following ways:

1. Joining together people from diverse social, cultural, economic, and geographic backgrounds

2. Preparing students for future leadership roles through

the vital leadership laboratory experience the arts offer for instilling discipline, planning, time management, teamwork, sales-marketing-consumer data mining, and trial and error

3. Constructing a gathering place for shared experiences that enrich the daily lives of students, faculty, and the community as only the arts can

4. Offering a once-in-a-lifetime opportunity for potential donors to awaken joy in thousands for generations to come while leaving a legacy in the community

5. Bringing new prospects for economic development to the area by collaborating with the School of Management in offering an arts and facilities management certificate program or academic area of emphasis within the university's growing undergraduate and increasingly international graduate programs

To paraphrase the wise words of leadership guru Warren Bennis: There are two ways of being creative. One can sing and dance. Or one can create an environment in which singers and dancers flourish. Leaders must encourage their organizations to dance to forms of music yet to be heard.[1]

14.
Leadership Family Business Methods

Herb Kelleher, founder of Southwest Airlines, once said that "the business of business is people."[1]

Early in my career, I was indeed fortunate to see this principle in action in the small Michigan town of Chelsea. Having been recruited away from the University of Michigan, I was a young, eager hospital vice president at a large, excellent, Catholic teaching facility owned and operated by the Religious Sisters of Mercy in Ann Arbor when I met Howard Holmes. Holmes was the CEO of the Chelsea Milling Company, an internationally renowned trailblazer in the packaged-food industry, and a member of the hospital board. The nature of my work was such that I met frequently with area business leaders, but none compared to this beloved and greatly admired leader of the company that makes Jiffy Mix products.

Howard Holmes and I met frequently for breakfast at Stivers, a small, unpretentious establishment off Interstate 94. We'd meet before 7 a.m., and I'm certain Howard had already put in a few hours at the mill before he met me.

During the course of nearly a decade of listening to and learning from him—and laughing with him as well—I formed my definition of the eight traits I believe make an inspiring, highly successful leader. Howard Holmes, of course, personified them all:

1. A genuine love of all people, including getting to know your employees so well they become an extension of your family

2. No disparity between what you say and what you do

3. A passion for success that is defined by doing what's right for your employees and your customers

4. Understanding that a corporate culture sets the context from which everything important evolves

5. A knack for bringing humor into the workplace and realizing that happy employees make for more satisfied customers and suppliers

6. A desire to recognize employees who take pride in their work and always remembering to celebrate their successes

7. An ability to speak in a clear, respectful, and straightforward manner

8. A humility that enables you to acknowledge mistakes and move on

Knowing that Howard's son, Howdy, had been named the Indianapolis 500 Rookie of the Year previously, I invited him to speak to our older son's Cub Scout den. I wanted to expose the youngsters to someone with the heart of a champion, and Howdy graciously agreed to meet with them. It was an evening I will never forget. Within a few minutes, he had captivated the group and they began sliding on their haunches across the gym floor to get closer and closer to him. As Howdy spoke about physical fitness, clean living, pursuing their dreams, and the importance of not making mistakes that could forever destroy their aspirations, I knew right then that this young man would become a truly inspiring leader. Howdy is "Midwest-friendly." He spoke to the children—not at them—was well organized, at times humorous, and clearly passionate about his message.

I have continued to follow the success of the Chelsea Milling Company albeit from a distance. I've done so not only because of our family's great admiration and personal fondness for the late Howard Holmes and his family, and not only because I relish many Jiffy Mix products (their brownie mix being the penultimate). I have done so because I remain a true believer in the personal values and business acumen of Howard "Howdy" Holmes, who in the mid-1990s succeeded his father as president and CEO.

Howdy is artfully perpetuating the rich 112-plus-year history of the Chelsea Milling Company as no one else could while making the adjustments and necessary changes required in a continuously turbulent and shifting business landscape.

15.
Leadership Home-Style

"Leadership is what you do at home."[1] Amway cofounder and NBA Orlando Magic owner Richard DeVos uttered this expression sometime ago.

I knew Rich when he was a trustee of the hospital where I was serving as senior vice president. A gifted leader who is certainly no stranger to adversity, Rich is a man of great faith, an indefatigable cheerleader, and an articulate and staunch champion of the free enterprise system.

My wife Joan and I received similar sage advice from our minister who married us many years ago. He advised us to model leadership in our lives, to read books on marriage and then discuss them, to never go to bed angry with each other, and to reach agreement on our respective life goals at the outset of our marriage. He was a firm believer that each one of us needed to make a 150 percent effort in order for our union to blossom and survive.

Neither of us used the term "leadership" to shape our discussion of the fundamentals of the kind of home we hoped to establish, nor was it used in either of our parents' homes. But leadership was more than abundant in both Joan's home and in mine even if it wasn't labeled as such. Joan and I established several ground rules that we would strive to live by:

- *Create our game plan (what many organizations typically refer to as their vision and strategy).* It consisted of a few planks: We wanted to live in a community where we could participate actively and where there existed heterogeneity, diversity, and a good college as lifelong learning was an integral part of our ethos. We wanted to get to know each other better before we started a family (four years into our marriage we embarked on this journey). And we made a commitment to share our experiences and our love with each other at the end of our respective workdays.

- *Set a high moral standard (what businesses often call their ethical stance).* We strived to set a high standard of regularly practicing our faith, remaining active in a denomination of our choosing when we began a family, and raising our children in the church as we believed it provided a key part of the foundation for a strong, healthy family.

- *Establish family traditions (what organizations sometimes call corporate culture).* We wanted to instill in our children an appreciation of people different from them, to broaden their and our knowledge of the arts, literature, and history, and to visit much of our own and other countries. It was important that our children learn self-discipline, respect for others, proper etiquette, and how to overcome adversity—experiencing life's "ups and downs" helps build strong character and resiliency. We also believed it was vital to our sons' development that they learn to love, have fun, be positive, be thankful for what they had, and assist others less fortunate.

- *Promote skills for success (what some businesses call structure, focus, and execution).* We believed that to reach their full potential our children needed to learn to be independent thinkers, self-sufficient, broad minded, and secular as well as sacred. We strived to expose them to people who were intellectually curious and well read, and whose views weren't necessarily the same as ours. We also wanted them to have heroes—people they had read about or had seen— who were inspiring, courageous, and worth looking up to. The complaint "Mom (or Dad), I'm bored" was never tolerated in our home and as a result was seldom heard.

We used books, Boy Scouts, athletics, concerts, reading to them, art galleries, lectures, travel to historic sites, close friends of various faiths, and numerous family discussions as ways to broaden our children's horizons and keep them occupied.

My wife comes from a family of three girls so I know it was a shock to her when we had two boys. But an even greater shock occurred when I learned she had been secretly studying the intricacies of football (and reading the sports pages), as it was one of three sports our sons played. She did so because she had decided if sports were one of their interests, she needed to become better informed. And I'll never forget when she shared a quote with me from Alabama's legendary head football coach, Paul "Bear" Bryant, which in a few words captured many of the lessons we tried to teach our children: "It's not the will to win that matters—everyone has that. It's the will to prepare to win that matters."[2]

Rich DeVos definitely knew what he was talking about when he said, "Leadership is what you do at home."[3] Leaders aren't born, they are made.

16.
Leadership, University Presidents, and the Bully Pulpit

The symbolic power of the campus president's voice is inestimable. The university president is arguably the most important position in the academic community. This role has evolved over many years from primarily an educator to an administrator position focused on ensuring the university's financial sustainability and developing its professional staff. Though changing, the president's role has always been influential and is responsible for the institution and the perpetuation of its values, as well as speaking on its behalf.

In 2010, we lost a great leader in Robben Fleming, who was, as president of the University of Michigan, a courageous spokesperson for racial justice and an ardent critic of the war in Vietnam. Fleming used his labor negotiation skills, patience, and humor to help the university weather that era without the destructive confrontations that affected other universities. Father Theodore Hesburgh was another impressive university president who led Notre Dame for 35 years. He received many awards for involving himself in battles about issues such as civil rights and immigration.

These public figures sought to defuse the Cold War, called for education reform, and urged higher moral standards for scientific research. But the high moral ground university presidents once held has been steadily weakened by numerous pressures affecting their positions, including conservative governing boards, insular student bodies and faculty, and shorter job tenures. Many are risk averse, leery of challenging the status quo and of offending regents, trustees, overseers, or directors.

They speak out about usual topics like proposed changes to the Higher Education Act or funding cuts to Pell Grants, but refrain from raising questions about unjust wars or defending civil liberties. They have too rarely taken issue with problems facing the nation or their regions and have too seldom "seized the bully pulpit" to address fiscal, environmental, or political concerns.

It is not hard to imagine why these leaders are no longer comfortable speaking out. Today's backlash to unpopular opinion is strong and immediate, partly because of the intense polarization of Americans on important issues. There is an angry division in this country that has manifested itself in many ways, including congressional gridlock. Fear of alienating partners and contributors might seem to go against other important goals like raising money and building partnerships. Any university leader who wishes to take a stand on issues that concern all Americans must be prepared to receive this backlash.

However daunting, standing up on these issues is crucial to leadership of a social institution such as a university. The university is sustained by its community and because of this cannot fail to be a vital force within it. It is privileged to have rich resources provided by government and the community, including the best minds in the country, large research holdings and endowments, committed support groups, and treasured academic freedom. It can draw from an arsenal of "think tanks" and successful alumni as well as close relationships with top corporations and foundations.

With such great and unique advantages, universities have a responsibility to identify and institutionalize civic and moral values and help cultivate a greater sense of integrity and community involvement.

Former USC President Steven Sample not only elevated USC as one of the nation's leading research institutions but also received national acclaim for forging unprecedented community partnerships. A university's president is expected to provide leadership for the institution's continued success. But leadership also entails developing students as future leaders and citizens who will challenge the present and enrich the future. The president's role must extend to helping solve the problems concerning all humans—the problems that many academic fields of study seek to answer.

It may be that the iconic, great college presidents who speak out to influence political issues of war, peace, and justice or authoring compelling, scholarly social works are a thing of the past. Yet, I am reminded of Pat McGuire who managed to rebuild Trinity Washington University during her two-decade-long tenure while speaking out on important topics that many of her peers wouldn't touch.

One can only hope other college presidents will follow the beacon that McGuire and others before her have illuminated for us all and demonstrate what real leaders are made of.

17.
Leadership and Marching Band Direction

Sometimes talent comes from unexpected places. Though our future business leaders are apt to come from top MBA programs or perhaps the military, these should not be the only avenues to search, especially when looking for leaders with a different point of view.

An often-overlooked arena for leadership development is the arts. Theater, music, and the fine arts all require, undeniably, an above-average level of creativity. But they also require the type of discipline, passion, and commitment that can be extremely valuable in many areas of business that are now floundering.

An excellent example of this is the marching band. I confess to being an avid football fan who thoroughly enjoys watching and listening to an excellent marching band during halftime shows at college games. Having had the good fortune of observing three giants in the collegiate ranks while in school—bandmasters Leonard Falcone of Michigan State University, William Revelli, and his successor George Cavender of the University of Michigan (who refined the "high step" and innovative uniform design)—I saw firsthand how they married their love of music with the highest standards of excellence and an uncanny ability to inspire college students, coupled with unremitting discipline.

Under Revelli's direction, the Michigan Marching Band was the first to use original scores for their band shows and employ synchronized music and movements. They were highly praised for their precision, formations, and style. Revelli was tough on his young band members and would not accept mediocrity in his organization. His exceptionally high standards called members to a higher commitment, not only to their music but also in all areas of their lives. He looked at the band as an antidote to juvenile delinquency.

The university's reputation as a premiere music institution is due in large part to Revelli's influence. Translating the same qualities he exhibited in rehearsals and on the field, and looking at how he pushed everyone in his band to reach for his or her greatest potential, there is no doubt that he would have made an excellent corporate leader had he chosen that path.

Los Angeles is also fortunate to have one of the greatest college marching bands in existence today, the USC Trojan Marching Band. Founded in 1880, it has made more than 350 consecutive game performances, numerous live appearances on

TV, in movies, at the Olympics, the Rose Bowl, the Academy Awards, and the Grammys, performed for several US presidents, and earned two platinum records. Interestingly, the band's conductor, Arthur Bartner, has all three of his academic degrees from the University of Michigan. His mentor in Ann Arbor was none other than William Revelli.

Then there is "The Band That Wouldn't Die."[1] In 1984, this self-supported, all-volunteer Baltimore Colts Marching Band, managed to work together and keep the band alive even after the Colts franchise was sold and moved to Indianapolis. The creativity, loyalty, and teamwork they showed are noteworthy, as is their story. In the wee hours of the morning when the Colts began their now infamous move to Indianapolis, band members managed to remove their equipment before the Mayflower moving vans arrived. What's more, they got their uniforms from the dry cleaners and hid them in a member's cemetery vault until the franchise gave them permission to keep them.

It was the band's incredible dedication and moxie over the next 12 years that helped convince the Maryland legislature to fund a new football stadium that eventually brought the Ravens franchise from Cleveland to Baltimore in 1996.

What specific leadership skills can we learn from these examples?

- Falcone, Revelli, and Cavender were excellent teachers who instilled pride and enthusiasm. They taught their band members how to attain excellence, even perfection, in performance, and how analysis, planning, goal setting, discipline, and love of the arts are lifetime skills, applicable to success in any endeavor.

- The USC Trojan Marching Band is recognized around the world for its organizational ability, ambassadorial skills, adaptability, and talent. These are traits to which all organizations should strive.

- The Baltimore Colts (now Ravens) Marching Band demonstrated how creativity, risk-taking, and fortitude can move obstacles, even when those obstacles seem insurmountable.

- The final, essential leadership quality seen in all these examples is passion. For the Colts Marching Band, it was a deep abiding loyalty and love for their city and for each other. For Falcone, Revelli, Cavender, and Bartner, it was a deep appreciation for what music can do, for tradition, innovation, teaching respect for authority, and for their beloved universities.

It's been said that "when work commitment and pleasure all become one and you reach that deep well where passion lives, nothing is impossible."[2] That's a good lesson for corporate America to learn and a good path to follow when searching for talent in different places. The future of many organizations may well depend on it.

18.
Embracing Diversity Makes
Good Business Sense

With the appointment to the US Supreme Court of "a Puerto Rican girl from the Bronx," as Justice Sonia Sotomayor described herself, the nation moved another step forward on that constitutional journey that strives "to form a more perfect union."[1]

There is something uniquely American in the way women and minorities, confronted with challenges and obstacles that sometimes seem unimaginable, can transform our society and make all Americans reexamine their core beliefs and long-held values.

Often, it takes brave leaders to show by example the real meaning of our Founding Fathers' belief that "all men are created equal" and that all Americans should have the opportunity to pursue their dreams and express their talents to the fullest potential.

In 1947, legendary Brooklyn Dodgers General Manager Branch Rickey exhibited both courage and savvy when he brought Jackie Robinson, the first African-American, to the major leagues. One of the first players to embrace Robinson was Hank Greenberg, a future Hall of Famer himself, who, by the time Robinson broke the color barrier, was playing for the Pittsburgh Pirates. As a Jew, Greenberg had endured extensive anti-Semitic verbal abuse and death threats throughout his career, so he knew firsthand the persecution and hatred Robinson was about to endure. No baseball player prior to Jackie Robinson's breaking the color barrier on April 15, 1947, had been subject to more abuse than Hank Greenberg. In the now famous story of how Greenberg rose to the occasion by lending "a helping hand" to Robinson on May 15, 1947, Stephen H. Norwood and Harold Brackman wrote:

> On May 15, 1947, in a game between the Pirates and the Dodgers, Robinson laid down a perfect bunt and streaked down the line to first. The pitcher's throw pulled first baseman Greenberg off the bag. Reaching for the throw, he collided with Robinson, who was able to get up and reach second. The next inning Greenberg walked, and asked Robinson, who was playing first base, if he had been hurt in the collision. Assured by Robinson that he hadn't been, Greenberg said to him, "Don't pay any attention to these guys who are trying to make it hard for you. Stick in there.... I hope you and I can get together for a talk. There are

a few things I've learned down through the years that might help you and make it easier."

Greenberg's support deeply moved Robinson and was widely praised in the African American press. Jackie told the *New York Times,* "Class tells. It sticks out all over Mr. Greenberg." Although Robinson suffered harassment unparalleled in baseball history, he recognized a kinship with what he called the "racial trouble" that Greenberg had also experienced. The *Pittsburgh Courier* reported that the Jewish slugger, who "many times...had [had] to close his ears when they hurled racial epithets at him from the opposing bench," definitely "understands Jackie's problems." The *Baltimore Afro-American* informed its readers that Greenberg, as "a Jew," was well-qualified to advise Robinson: "The more pressure you're under, the better ball player you'll become—I know."

African American sportswriter Wendell Smith suggested that, had the collision involved a player other than Greenberg, it might have sparked a riot.[2]

In a similar way, businessmen and women who bear the burden of overcoming bias or racism due to their gender, ethnicity, or skin color must be allowed to prove their worth and pursue their dreams through their performance in corporate America. If given the chance, they can help to create a more diverse, just, and vibrant workplace while inspiring others to do great things.

The sad reality, however, is that while women and minorities may be able to "get through the door" more easily than their parents or grandparents, too often they still must confront some of the ugly obstacles that challenged Robinson and Greenberg more than 60 years ago.

If a white male had been nominated for the Supreme Court seat now occupied by Sotomayor, it is highly unlikely that his hearing would have focused as much on his "feelings" and his "personal experiences" (notwithstanding the president's remarks) or how his gender and ethnicity might "bias" his interpretation and application of the law.

But stereotypes still exist and, as Greenberg demonstrated by his actions, it is only by creating a level playing field that the best and the brightest will have the opportunity to prevail.

The July 2009 issue of *Harvard Business Review* carried an article by Ronald Heifetz entitled "Leadership in a (Permanent) Crisis." In it, he and his coauthors remind us that "to generate new leadership and innovative ideas, you need to leverage diversity."[3]

Organizations that employ people with the widest range of life experiences, views, and dissimilar backgrounds will be more adaptive and successful in an increasingly global and competitive economy.

It makes sound business sense to embrace diversity fully at all levels of an organization. Such inclusion will promote much-needed commitment from the organization's entire workforce and, in so doing, enhance an institution's reputation and public image. But more than that, it is simply the right thing to do.

19.
Leadership Wake-Up Call:
The Millennials

The first generation to be brought up with the technological revolution is entering America's workforce. Are they overindulged, demanding, accustomed to instant gratification, impatient? This may be true to some extent, but this new blood has the potential to transform the world of business in new and valuable ways.

The first wave of Millennials, or so-called Generation Y, born roughly between 1980 and 2001, is already making its presence felt. It's estimated that more than 58 million of them will be employed by 2014.

Contrary to the opinions of some business professionals, there is much promise emanating from these Nexters who will be relied upon to improve American ingenuity, innovation, and competitiveness in an increasingly global marketplace. Despite the impression many of us have of them, Millennials will contribute a whole host of talents going forward:

- They are bright, industrious, and driven to success.

- They want to be challenged and given more regular feedback on their performance so they can chart the improvement required.

- They are technologically savvy, cross-culturally aware, and committed to sustainability and diversity.

- They are not as trusting of corporate titans and politicians, and are not afraid to question the status quo.

- They are the most civic-minded generation to come along in some time. Volunteering is a priority for many of them as they strive to make the world a better place to live.

Millennials will alter most businesses and institutions as we know them today. Organizations that embrace them will reap the rewards, and organizations that stick with the status quo will be left in the dust. Accustomed to high achievement throughout high school and college, Millennials will gravitate toward organizations that provide frequent performance appraisals, give periodic positive feedback at the successful conclusion of a project, assign "mentors," and offer flex-time. It is important to remember that many of these individuals will complete their work assignments at nontraditional times (often in the evening or early morning hours).

Organizations that embrace the parents of these young workers will be more successful in recruiting and retaining them. Parents have played a very influential, close, personal role in the development of these Millennials. Ron Alsop, in *The Trophy Kids Grow Up,* cites Ogilvy Worldwide as a firm that demonstrates understanding of the importance parents play by sponsoring a program like "Parents Day at the Office," and notes that IBM and FedEx are wise to encourage parents to tour their offices or attend receptions.

Organizations that genuinely engage this generation, recognize their need for positive reinforcement, give them greater responsibility early on, set limits, and articulate their expectations at the outset will likely experience fewer turnovers than more traditional, hierarchical, and less-flexible organizations.

Millennials want to work, but for companies that have an "edge" over others. They seek growth opportunities and advancement sooner than their predecessors. Thus, organizations that commit the necessary resources to construct their own internal talent engine will more often be selected by this group.

It is critically important that organizations motivate their young workforce by closely connecting their job, company success, and career development in a fully integrated way.

Through teaching and supervising Millennials, I have found them to be energizing, passionate, intelligent, and, yes, at times exasperating. But what they may sometimes lack in etiquette, they more than make up for with energy, creativity, drive to succeed, and their true dedication to making the world a better place.

20.
What Organzations Can Learn from Reading Military Résumés

Amerca's organizations are missing out on a great pool of men and women in uniform who have demonstrated ability for innovation, dependability, loyalty, and risk-taking beyond their years. This is largely because recruiters and business leaders simply don't know how to interpret military résumés. It may come as little surprise given the sharp decline in the number of chief executive officers, working media, and even members of Congress who possess military experience.

But what better source can organizations tap than the military to recruit men and women with sophisticated, quantitative, analytical, logistical, and operational skills; demonstrated flexibility honed by having faced life-and-death situations; experience overcoming practically every form of adversity, and knowledge gained by leading and motivating others and excelling with major responsibilities?

Marines, soldiers, airmen, sailors, and coast guardsmen frequently have impressive résumés documenting their composure and clear thinking under fire, proven leadership ability under harsh conditions, supervisory experience, and dedication and resolve to succeed that are not easy to find.

Since the beginning of the Iraq war, young Marines and soldiers, in order to achieve their missions, have had to multitask by assuming such diverse leadership roles as distributing food, leading patrols, negotiating among feuding neighbors, and engaging in major firefights. Unfortunately, however, business leaders are largely unprepared to fully comprehend how these kinds of real-life experiences translate into value within a business organization.

Perhaps they need to dig just a bit deeper. Often, the military résumé is written in a format unfamiliar to a recruiter who has no experience with the military. The résumé may contain military terms a recruiter is not familiar with.

If recruiters merely took the time to find out what the résumé really says about the individual, they might find the best person for the job is staring them right in the face. Here are some tips recruiters can use to effectively recognize the talents and skills of military personnel, and how they can be applied to their organizations:

- Examine the various assignments the veteran has completed. The junior Marine or soldier can often organize, analyze, and execute tasks quickly, efficiently, and with scarce resources and little oversight.

- Examine the detail-oriented roles the serviceman or woman has performed and for whom. They have often conceived strategies and implemented tactics similar to city managers, mayors, or business executives when collaboration with others is required for a successful business venture.

- Scrutinize the financial numbers of the assets delegated to this person during deployment. They may have valuable experience handling equipment typically costing millions of dollars to operate and repair. This is a significant responsibility that has great value in business operations.

- In the interview, ask how he or she was able to lead a large contingent of soldiers, sailors, or Marines. This kind of management experience is invaluable now more than ever to bring out innovative methods that can be used to beat the competition effectively.

- Explore how the veteran has dealt both with ambiguity and structure. There is little question veterans often bring a greater maturity, self-confidence, and stronger work ethic to the business arena than many MBAs with no prior military or civilian work experience.

If the résumé is presented in an unfamiliar format or contains military terms or acronyms, do not hesitate to have the person explain whatever it is you do not understand. You may find this information reveals a lot about the person's experience, and knowing these terms will help in screening other applicants with military backgrounds. As a bonus, that explanation will give you a greater sense of the person's communication skills.

The ability of Israeli businesses to recognize the value of military experience in their organizations is described by Dan Senor and Saul Singer in their 2009 book *Start-Up Nation: The Story of Israel's Economic Miracle*: "Israel boasts the highest density of start-ups in the world and has more companies listed on the NASDAQ than companies from all over Europe. In 2008, per-capacity venture capital investments in Israel were 2.5 times greater than in the U.S."[1]

Israel has produced more start-up companies than India, China, Japan, South Korea, Canada, and the United Kingdom.

One of the significant factors cited by Senor and Singer for this success is the high premium Israel's leaders place on military experience when recruiting new employees. If business leaders want serious, mature new hires who have the ability to deal with myriad situations, work as productive team players, and who possess valuable real-world experience, they should look deeper into the military résumé and see what a great wealth of experience lies on that page.

"Never doubt that a small group of thoughtful committed citizens can change the world."®
—Margaret Mead

SECTION III

Leadership Is Not a
Solo Flight

21.
The Value of Stakeholders

It is sometimes easy to lose track of the fundamentals that provide the anchor to our success, a safety net in times of crisis, and a compass to guide our decision making. The 2004 standoff in Ventura, California, between Community Memorial Hospital's administration and board versus physicians brings to mind some fundamental truths.

One of the fundamentals that I have seen eroding over the last decade is appreciation for the importance of physicians. It is easy to make physicians the butt of our amusement—to exploit the stereotypes of enormous egos and unabashed arrogance. With the exception of lawyers, there have probably been more jokes told about doctors than about any other group of professionals.

But while physicians may be easy prey for late-night comics, we must recognize that it is to our benefit for hospitals and government representatives to take the time to work closely with physicians.

In general, doctors are well read, educated, concerned, articulate, knowledgeable, and, despite reports to the contrary, surprisingly accessible. They provide invaluable input to our healthcare planning, perspective to our thinking, and feedback on how our ideas are working.

They can help sell an idea to other healthcare providers and insurers and credibly express a hospital's position to the media and the community. Most physicians that I have encountered realize that their own success is closely linked to the success of a hospital or other healthcare facility.

It is a cliché that nobody admits himself or herself into a hospital. But, sometimes, clichés ring true. Hospitals do not admit patients directly. Unlike nearly every other commercial enterprise, healthcare requires a third party to engage the transaction between the patient and the hospital. That third party is the doctor. Physicians admit the patients, they discharge the patients, and they—along with dedicated nurses and other professionals—hold in their hands the key to the satisfactory outcome of a patient's stay in the hospital.

Plainly stated, without physicians hospitals are out of business. So, if for no other reason than one of pragmatism, it is in the best interest of hospital administrators and trustees to work closely with doctors in a collaborative fashion and to integrate them as much as possible into the hospital's business. The success of any organization depends on the commitment of all stakeholders, including physicians.

The argument for this is so obvious that I am continuously baffled as to why some hospital administrators view physicians not as part of their team but almost as adversaries. I am not implying that all hospitals have that philosophy, but plenty do.

As I reflect on more than 20 years in healthcare marketing and public affairs, it is abundantly clear that those who took the time to mentor me, sprinkle my days with optimism, and instill the highest calling of ethical standards were physicians. At teaching hospitals and academic medical centers from Michigan to Indiana to Stanford, it has been physicians I've most enjoyed being around and who have been the most helpful to my own career.

I don't kid myself though. I am not in their fraternity, have no MD after my name, and know that I will never be a full-fledged member in their club. I'm not even sure I want to be. But I do want to be respected by the members of this noble fraternity, and I know that desire comes from having taken the time as an administrator to cultivate relationships and involve them whenever possible. It just makes good business sense to include an integral part of your organization in the decision-making process beyond lip service.

From strategic planning to tactical execution, organizations need to be aware of the tremendous reservoir of talent, knowledge, and energy that go untapped because not all stakeholders are part of the process. In this scenario, everyone loses: the organization, the patients, the employees, and the shareholders (if any). Organizational leaders, including hospitals and trustees, should go back to the fundamentals and try reconnecting with their stakeholders. They just might like the results.

22.
Leadership by Fiat Never Works

Having been on an extensive trip to Poland and other parts of Central Europe, I was anxious to read Zbigniew Brzezinski's book *Strategic Vision* when I arrived home. As I read it, my mind wandered to several organizations seemingly lacking a vision that engages people and doesn't enrage them. While Brzezinski makes a compelling case for unity, solving our domestic problems, and a broader vision for international relations, his advocacy for leaders to practice engagement is not surprising given his distinguished record in government, higher education, and corporate board service.

Another book by the Polish-born former US National Security Advisor and Johns Hopkins University professor, *Totalitarian Dictatorship and Autocracy,* drew a likeness between the Catholic Church and Communism from another time in our history.

Although decades have passed since the heyday of Communism, suppression of dissent and discrimination are unfortunately alive and well in some business environs and certainly in the Catholic Church. Congress has gotten into the act by passing legislation to protect whistle-blowers while the Catholic Church has taken the opposite position. It is apparent in the Vatican's April 2012 decree proclaiming that US Catholic nuns spend less time on critical matters of social justice and poverty and be more outspoken in opposing abortion, contraception, and same-sex marriage.

While I'm hardly an expert on the Catholic Church, I do believe I know a thing or two about leadership and the sisters. I had the distinct pleasure of working with the Religious Sisters of Mercy for many years in a large Catholic hospital where I witnessed their ministry firsthand. They are the most caring, intelligent, industrious, and thoughtful community I've encountered in my career. The selfless work of nuns from all Catholic orders in inner-city soup kitchens, domestic violence shelters, hospitals, free clinics, and schools around the world is unparalleled. Their dedication to effectively dealing with poverty, helping oppressed and powerless people, and combating the worst global diseases imaginable is truly remarkable. They really are the "public face" of the Catholic Church. It has often been said that they do the actual work of God, not simply preach it.

The Vatican reprimand, apparently based on little dialogue with the nuns themselves, appears to be one more effort being exerted by the male-dominated hierarchy—especially many US priests, the Conference of Catholic Bishops, and the Holy See—to silence the nuns and get them in line. To the male hierarchy of the Church, I suggest they reconsider their blatant, dictatorial power play by practicing three essential leadership qualities:

1. Meet with and listen to the nuns' points of view developed from their centuries of work in the trenches.

2. Show respect for these female leaders by ceasing the demeaning, disrespectful, and cowardly issuance of decrees that harken back to tyrants all too familiar to us.

3. Abandon the reckless use of authority by genuinely trying to collaborate with and honor the devotion and longstanding, courageous service of the nuns.

Good communication, respect for others, being receptive to advice from those who work tirelessly with those in need, and collaboration are among the basic qualities of successful leadership in any organization, be it corporate, religious, or political.

In my book *Real Leaders Don't Boss* I write that effective leaders don't put obstacles in front of people; they help remove them. Let us hope that the Vatican, which represents one of the largest organizations in the world, will soon practice engagement through greater freedom, openness, and appreciation, not hostility, toward women religious.

Continuing to rule by top-down fiat with little or no discussion is demeaning and counterproductive. It is the antithesis of enlightened leadership in any organization and a very bad habit! Church leaders might heed Dwight D. Eisenhower's words of wisdom: "You do not lead by hitting someone over the head—that's assault, not leadership." [1] It is disappointing that Pope Francis has reaffirmed his predecessor's reprimand.

23.
Corporate Culture Counts

Corporate America has had no shortage of legends: Kellogg, Hewlett, Disney, Packard, Kroc, Watson, Ash, Grove, and Iacocca. These leaders come to mind as examples of lions who have emblazoned their names as corporate giants. Many wonder how history will treat the likes of such Silicon Valley titans as Google's Page, Zynga's Pincus, Facebook's Zuckerberg, and some of the other Internet pioneers. But far more important than heroic reputations are the values these leaders personified and instilled within their organizations.

When reading the news these days, I sometimes wonder if we have completely forgotten the tenets these giants used to shape American industry. While it is true that history can both illuminate and obfuscate, we would do well to remember the past in the case of these great examples.

Several years ago, I had the privilege of spending a summer at Abbott Laboratories north of Chicago as a PhRMA Fellow. While there I observed a wide array of Abbott executives, scientists, and managers. I was struck not only by their disciplined approach but also by their freedom to discover, develop, and design within broad operating parameters—conditions I did not typically associate with large, for-profit corporations. It was there that I first became fascinated with the question, What makes a successful organization?

As a manager "on loan" to Abbott from the University of Michigan, I quickly found similarities between the two organizations. While it may be better known to some for its legendary football, winged helmets, and "Hail to the Victors" fight song, Michigan, much like Abbott Laboratories, is one of the world's premier research institutions where scientific rigor, intellectual freedom, and disciplined scholarship thrive in a lively, entrepreneurial, and decentralized university environment. I realized then that the same core principles could apply regardless of industry.

Perhaps the most crucial link connecting great leaders and their vision is the personal value system they demonstrate and teach to others that becomes ingrained in the fabric of the firm, the so-called corporate culture. Today's best leaders realize that a strong corporate culture is the glue that unites people and provides them with a raison d'etre that's bigger than any product or service. Profit is necessary, but it shouldn't be the paramount goal. Results from a seven-year study conducted by the Workplace Research Foundation and University of Michigan investigator

Palmer Morrel–Samuels, PhD, confirmed that as employee morale improves a firm's stock price enjoys higher returns.[1]

Undeniably, today's global marketplace is a far cry from the insular corporate environment of the past. Perhaps two of the biggest barriers today to establishing and perpetuating an enduring corporate culture are:

- Excessive CEO and executive compensation packages, reflective of greed and a short-term mind-set

- A workforce composed of increasing numbers of younger employees who do not often remain at a company for more than a few years

When a widening gulf in salaries and benefits between the top and bottom ranks of an organization exceeds acceptable bounds, employees are less likely to feel a need to work harder, let alone possess the sense of loyalty, responsibility, and trust needed to help solve a company's most pressing challenges. They will often point to the C-suite where executive perks and bonuses are out of control and say "Let *them* solve it!" As companies have had to cut costs to survive and, as a result, expect remaining employees to pick up the slack, the disparity in compensation has become a battle cry across the business landscape that is also reverberating in the halls of Congress.

The younger workforce presents challenges as well. This generation is far less enamored by traditional organizations and is more independent than any that came before. They can pose major challenges for today's managers, especially if those managers are part of a different generation. New forms of stimulus and incentives should be created to appeal to these technologically savvy, bright, and environmentally conscious young minds. Presenting more stimulating assignments, frequent two-way dialogue, and company-supported affinity groups can help achieve this.

The values of many former great leaders were forged by the experiences of the Great Depression, the World Wars, and humble beginnings. They understood the impact that a strong, adaptive corporate culture has on organizational performance, the true mark of leadership.

They treated workers as their greatest asset, investing in and motivating them. They understood that the purpose of business was to serve the customer. They expected high standards for employee behavior that they themselves modeled and reinforced.

Perhaps if today's business leaders took a page from history, their companies would achieve the success created by the enlightened leadership of past corporate giants. And that would be a good thing.

24.
Pride and Loyalty: Motivating Your Team

There are five specific ways to build pride and loyalty at work (and I would add at home, too). What may be most surprising is that none of these are ground-breaking concepts but instead are time-tested actions based on my own experience:

1. Personally deliver handwritten notes to team members who have done a particularly exemplary job (for example, after completing a major project that resulted in securing a new contract or surpassing revenue expectations), are experiencing a particularly difficult challenge such as a personal health issue or family crisis, or are celebrating an important milestone (for example, a company or individual anniversary, a christening, or a Bar or Bat Mitzvah).

   Rationale: Leaders who regularly demonstrate their

93

humanity, humility, and genuine interest in their associates' well-being inspire others, thus contributing immeasurably to a positive organizational culture. The key to writing thoughtful, succinct personal notes is not to do them too often but on special occasions as noted above.

2. Listen, learn, and lead as you mingle with people in your organization. By listening carefully to your associates, you demonstrate a sincere interest in them and their work; by learning their names you demonstrate that they are important to you and the organization. Effective leaders frequently send an e-mail or place a telephone call a few days after meeting a new employee or learning something new about their current employees. The best leaders will tell you that it is time well spent.

    Rationale: Many authors write about what are often leadership fads or gimmicks. But today's workers appreciate leaders who are competent, connected, caring, and committed people of character and serve them and their organization. Imagine how many employees tell their coworkers that their leader called them or sent them an e-mail a few days after some interaction on the shop floor, the hospital ward, or in their cubicle?

3. Remove obstacles that inhibit progress toward attainment of team goals, but also know when to get out of the team's way. Effective leaders are connected with their employees but have the wisdom to know when not to interfere. If the team is struggling and can't seem to find daylight after

several attempts, the leader sometimes needs to take steps to remove a seemingly impenetrable obstacle, but only after conferring with the team leader or the entire team.

Rationale: Real leaders know when to lead from the front but also realize the importance of fully empowering the team and not micromanaging them. It is an art that well-connected leaders master from experience.

4. A well-coordinated, effectively led special event can frequently build significant goodwill inside an organization while concomitantly strengthening its brand and growing its business externally. Too often, special events are treated as frills and perceived as a one-time, independent, unrelated goal. Rather, they should be planned as a frugal, interrelated, and integral part of an organization's mission, culture, and strategic plan. A thoughtful special event bolsters employees' pride in their organization, enables them to feel good about themselves, and draws outside constituencies closer inside the tent.

Rationale: Special events are often not given their just due when it comes to the very positive impact they can have on employee pride and loyalty and their overall positive impact on the company's reputation enhancement agenda. Real leaders understand their leverage in the workplace.

5. Establish an emotional connection with workers by ensuring you often let them know the following:

   • They are important, needed, and valued; there are many appropriate ways to accomplish this.

- When you are wrong, let them know you were in error—don't be afraid to apologize as it is a sign of strength, not weakness as some believe.

- Be positive, cheerful, and upbeat; we tend to gravitate to people who are optimistic. More often than not, this condition is contagious in the best way.

25.
What Teams Can Learn
from Teams

Many years have passed since legendary Michigan football coach Bo Schembechler exhorted his Wolverines in a rousing pregame pep talk to execute according to his motto, "The Team, The Team, The Team."[1] His was an inspirational reminder about unselfish play, players believing in one another, their resolve to encourage each other, and their shared goal of winning a championship above individual aspirations.

David Brandon, former Domino's Pizza chairman and CEO and current athletic director at Michigan, played for Coach Schembechler. Brandon said, "Great team players will compete when they are tired and hurting because their team needs them."[2]

The Olympics reminds us of teams and what they can do. One team that comes to mind was the remarkable group known as "the Dream Team," the gold-medal-winning 1992 US Olympic men's basketball team. Friends had remarked to me that they succeeded because they had the best talent, with the likes of Jordan, Magic, Bird, "The Admiral," Barkley, and Malone.

No one can rightfully argue that this group wasn't supremely skilled, but I believe their success was largely due to their having jelled as a team and to enlightened coaching. The chemistry and the play-making Magic Johnson and Larry Bird fostered were pivotal as they helped transform a group of established all-stars into a team whose members forgot themselves and supported each other.

For a good lesson on teamwork, writer Jim Vesterman describes his experience as college-student-turned-Marine as an exercise in depending on others and being depended upon, not only for survival in the field but also for success in achieving goals. Vesterman concludes, "In many ways, there's probably no better preparation I could have had for the business world than joining the Marine Corps. The Marines teach you how to be both a leader and a follower." [3]

Though there is no tried-and-true recipe to build a winning team, in my first book, *Real Leaders Don't Boss*, I cite several examples of leaders whose methods, if tailored to the particular group, can positively influence desired outcomes. Five of the most important of these include:

1. Explain clearly and confidently where you intend to lead the group and the role each person will play to maximize the team's success. To do this, you must know

each member of your group well and have fully assessed their strengths and weaknesses.

2. Evaluate regularly the performance of each person, chart how he or she can improve, and candidly share his or her progress.

3. Teach the group to be unselfish, to be honest with themselves and their teammates, to share, to be enthusiastic and committed to group success. Mold them into a team characterized by each person feeling responsible to one another—not to the supervisor, coach, or organization.

4. Be a person of high integrity and live according to your ethical standards. Always set an enviable example, use praise generously, and when constructive criticism is required, give it without embarrassing the person. Such a foundation is needed to establish and maintain a group's genuine respect over time.

5. Celebrate like families do. Teach what it feels like to succeed as a group and your team will be motivated to work together.

Many years ago, my father took our family to the old Kezar Stadium in San Francisco to watch the 49ers play the Chicago Bears. When the Bears—then led by head coach George "Papa Bear" Halas—entered the stadium that afternoon, the noise of the crowd was louder than all the foghorns in the Bay Area combined.

As is the case with many sports trailblazers whom business leaders try to emulate today, Coach Halas emphasized many of the same principles shared by Schembechler, John Wooden, Bobby Knight and his protégé Mike Krzyzewski, Pat Riley, and others: strict discipline, solid fundamentals, relentless execution, and a lifelong bond among players and coaches.

In the end, success in every walk of life requires a true team effort. And few pleasures are more meaningful than participating as part of something bigger than ourselves. As Coach Halas once remarked, "Nobody who ever gave his best regretted it."[4]

26.
Building a Better Board

Having served as a hospital executive, trustee, and board chair of both not-for-profit and for-profit hospitals and health systems in the Midwest and West, my experience suggests that other than having major friction with the medical staff, nothing can undermine the CEO faster than disillusioned or frustrated board members.

How often have you pondered the following questions as you're heading home after a less-than-productive board meeting: Why doesn't the president and CEO better utilize board members? Why aren't some of the new directors (trustees) young adults who reflect the growing and important digital dynamic, multitasking approach to the business world? Why are the "leaders of yesterday" often being selected to fill seats in the boardroom instead of the "leaders of tomorrow"?

There is no doubt that the time has come to more fully utilize the expertise represented by hundreds of thousands of young community leaders who currently give unselfishly of their time, talent, and even treasure to serve as board members of important organizations. This sense of urgency is heightened by the necessity to expand our existing board ranks by enlisting the youngest "best and brightest" from the wired world—people who can more effectively make use of the latest technologies to improve procedures and expand the organization's outreach. Here are four principal ways you can help address the issue:

1. When you are asked to join a board or suggest names of board candidates, ask the president and CEO if he or she truly intends to tap the expertise of new board members. But don't stop there. Since the response (genuine or not) is most likely to be "yes," ask specifically how he or she plans to accomplish this goal.

2. Point out that since most organizations schedule somewhere between four to eight board meetings a year that last two to three hours each, how else, outside of board meetings, will members' skills in such areas as customer service, mergers and acquisitions, branding, media relations, producing financial results, investing—to name a few—be harnessed? Are newer members teamed up with more experienced board members to more quickly grasp the mission of the organization and their role in it? Are member expectations made clear and is accountability monitored? Is there a well-developed board orientation program?

3. Then, if you're satisfied with the responses, ask if the organization's leader has considered going "outside the box" to recruit young, bright, enterprising professionals for at least a few of the available board seats. When he or she pauses to consider your question, quickly ask if he or she realizes how young people are often poles apart from you both in how they approach today's business problems and how distinctly they engage in critical thinking and process challenges. In other words, ask how high a value he or she places on hearing diverse, generational points of view before making decisions.

4. If you conclude that you are on the same wavelength, pose these $64,000 questions: What role does he or she see the board playing in setting strategy? Is the board going to be more involved than it was a year ago? Does he or she encourage the board to discuss strategy during dinner before the meeting actually convenes? Is the primary role of the board to help set the overall strategy for the organization?

As we all know, the best CEOs want the best boards and they also want the best possible board relationships. Too often, however, there is disparity in how the CEO sees the board functioning and how an individual board member wants to be utilized. The result is frequently underutilized or misused human capital, which can lead to frustration and potential conflict in the boardroom and beyond.

If you ask these questions and others that occur to you, I can assure you that you will have a better idea of how much the president or CEO wants the board to be involved in true governance and what kind of board he or she genuinely wants. And, you can hopefully help improve how your board functions, thus enhancing your organization's success.

"The best leader understands the power of unleashing individual talent by offering persons the opportunity to learn, to be enterprising and to make a contribution."

—Dr. Clifton R. Wharton, Jr.

SECTION IV

Leaders Don't Grow on Trees

27.
Nothing Beats a Strong Bench
for Future Leaders

As a young person, I played several sports. Like many of my generation, if I didn't have a glove, bat, or ball of some kind in my hand most of the time—whether it was a football, baseball, basketball, or tetherball (and they were very rarely new!)—something felt amiss.

I was fortunate in that once I became involved in organized sports, I played a lot. I also confess to having spent some time getting splinters (in you know where!) from occasionally riding the bench. Yet even that experience was valuable.

As I got older, John Havlicek of the Boston Celtics became one of my heroes, as did his incomparable coach, Red Auerbach, for his skillful development and use of his bench. But my focus here is a slightly different type of bench.

The Leadership Pipeline

Most of us are familiar with organizations like General Electric, IBM, Procter & Gamble, the US Marine Corps, and Federal Express. What makes these companies successful? They have long realized that in order to be successful year after year, they must consciously and continuously strengthen their leadership pipeline—and grow their pool of future leaders from within.

Unfortunately, many organizations of similar and even smaller size do not yet see the value of a CEO who sees his or her most critical role as that of teacher or mentor.

The Urgency of Effective Leadership

We live in a world that is continuously changing. As such, it requires that we identify and develop effective leadership more rapidly.

To quote change expert John Kotter, "As we transition to a world where change is continuous—not episodic—urgency must become a core, sustained capability."[1] Our focus should be to take immediate steps to encourage senior leaders to act with this sense of urgency. Our leaders should also be actively involved as advisers and counselors of younger talent at every level of their companies and expect their direct reports to do the same.

For those executives who say, "I'd love to but I'm just too busy," I encourage them to recall that legendary leader of General Electric Jack Welch probably spent more time on this one responsibility than any other during his long tenure. It's time for leaders to start teaching leadership.

Developing a Leader Pipeline

Two immediate and pragmatic actions must be undertaken in order to develop a leadership pipeline.

First, organizations must commit to teaching managers how to become leaders. The need for such resolute commitment should be obvious: presidents, CEOs, and members of the leadership team who take time to train and guide their lieutenants ultimately experience more success in driving operating performance.

Of equal benefit is that employee retention is heightened while costs are lessened in organizations that effectively leverage the talent of their staffs. Another upside is that executives who instruct others often become great leaders themselves.

The second requirement is for executives to deliberately develop a corporate culture and an education structure that builds future leaders from within. For many organizations, it often seems more expedient to hire young talent from "known" entities—such as top academic institutions like Harvard, Stanford, Michigan, Chicago, or Berkeley; stalwart companies like Boeing, Ritz-Carlton, Apple, Southwest, or Microsoft; or the military.

Other companies spend precious capital to retain teams from top-shelf consulting firms like McKinsey, Bain, Boston Consulting, Booz & Company, AT Kearney, and others. While doing so often leads to short-term success, such recruiting strategies rarely deliver lasting results and true business innovation.

The central spoke of a winning organization should be internally developed leaders who understand the company's business strategy along with its culture—people who possess the internal credibility to drive insightful change and quality performance.

Today's workplace suffers no shortage of so-called leaders-in-waiting—young people hoping to be identified, mentored, challenged, and developed by senior leadership. The problem is a company's unwillingness to make the investment in people, both young and older. Can you imagine if Fred Smith didn't believe that the people of FedEx were the bedrock of their present and future business success?

As Tichy and Cohen have written: "The job of the leader has not changed. Enhancing the value of the assets and sustaining growth are still the ultimate goals. This is accomplished by developing others to be leaders at every level and getting them aligned and energized."[2]

We would do well to heed the admonition by Peter Drucker: "Be a teacher. Rank does not confer privilege or give power. It imposes responsibility."[3] Can you think of a more profound legacy to leave your organization than a robust leadership pipeline?

28.
Small Wins and Broken Windows

My father was a teacher, coach, and later a school principal in Northern California from the 1940s through the 1970s. He was one of those who firmly believed in the separate theories of "small wins" and "broken windows" before they were formally advanced by such scholars as Karl Weick, James Q. Wilson, and George Kelling.

Weick stated that if people can see small, visible, and steady changes being made in an organization, this experience would help reduce resistance to larger change efforts being introduced.[1]

The "broken windows" theory postulated by Kelling and Wilson held that if you quickly repaired damaged facilities— broken windows—you could prevent further destructive acts.[2] Both theories have been subject to debate among academics, producing different schools of thought regarding their validity.

I suspect that because my dad had such success with his own personal blend of these two practices in his career as an educator, especially in teaching mathematical reasoning and sports techniques, it was only natural that I would adopt them into my own career. As a naval officer and later as a hospital and university executive, I found these two theories particularly useful when participating in organizational change initiatives. They have worked well for me in several major ways.

Improving Organizational Culture

The foremost quality required by an effective leader is the ability to inspire others to recognize the need to alter the ways things have been done historically. Through the learned skill of storytelling, the leader converts a few like-minded people who soon capture the leader's vision. They, in turn, begin to chart a course to win over a new cast of "true believers." As the new believers begin to implement a small number of successful changes (victories or "small wins") they slowly but surely enlist a growing band of new leaders who do likewise.

While working at a large hospital, I applied this principle to the area of improving customer service, learning to preserve the best of the existing culture while building new platforms aided by new technologies that would better differentiate the hospital in the marketplace—all the while always remembering to staunchly support the preeminence of the patient-physician relationship.

Instilling Newly Found Pride in the Organization

There are many ways to build pride in any organization. When I was faced with this challenge working for a private university, I believed that a good place to start was with the physical appearance of the campus.

My belief was that if I could eliminate faded signs, outdated landscaping, chipped and peeling paint, rust, and broken concrete walks, I would gradually arouse the workforce so they would come forward to offer new ideas that would make the organization a more attractive and productive environment.

By utilizing a cross-functional team for change with representatives from numerous departments and including both faculty and trustees, I found I could make and execute decisions better and more quickly. This approach often leads to enhanced worker performance, greater pride in people and their surroundings, and a greatly improved reputation for the organization. As my father put it: "If the place looks good, people will think it's good."

Driving to a Better Future

I also learned early in my career that too much bureaucracy stifles ingenuity, creativity, and originality. It also thwarts leadership development unless you find that rare organization where teaching new leaders has long been an integral part of the organizational fabric. Perhaps most importantly, too much bureaucracy often gives the workforce a false sense of security and reluctance to change.

As chief of marketing and public affairs, I often teamed with others to raise the organization's consciousness that the world is changing rapidly and that we needed to be more nimble, responsive, and adaptable. As Howdy Holmes, mentioned earlier in this book, said: "Rewards come from growing, not standing still. Once you reach your destination, if you don't set out on another trip, you're stranded."[3]

Leading or participating in a change effort is most likely to get someone's dander up. If it doesn't, it is highly probable that the change isn't significant enough. Change initiatives are not, therefore, for the weak or timid.

Machiavelli may have had it right when he wrote: "There is nothing more difficult to carry out, nor more doubtful of success, nor more dangerous to handle, than to initiate a new order of things."[4]

29.
Leadership Lessons from Capitol Hill

Every US president has had to contend with vociferous critics from both sides of the political continuum. It is the nature of the beast.

Franklin D. Roosevelt, for example, faced many domestic threats to his agenda in the persons of a Detroit priest, the Rev. Charles E. Coughlin, and Louisiana Sen. Huey "Kingfish" Long, among others. Ronald Reagan had to cope with journalist Strobe Talbott and Massachusetts Sen. Ted Kennedy, who vigorously opposed his approach to foreign policy.

Fast-forward to the recent past where US Sens. John McCain and Lindsey Graham rapidly became the two most frequent, outspoken opponents of many of President Obama's initiatives.

If their criticism were directed only to the president's policies, their views would carry the gravitas worthy of their elected positions and would trigger the kind of healthy debate that is critical in a democracy. Sadly, however, their rancor was increasingly directed to other public servants in the current administration and appeared designed to restrict the President's hand in nominating potential members of his second-term Cabinet.

As a former naval officer, I have long admired Sens. McCain and Graham not only for their dedicated military and civilian service but also for having the courage of their convictions, regardless of how the public winds may blow.

However, their comments concerning the possible nomination of UN Ambassador Susan Rice as secretary of state struck me as being beyond the pale. Ambassador Rice performed admirably in her role at the United Nations, and premature allegations, outlandish intentions to block her nomination, and calls for a Watergate-like investigation into the attack on the US Consulate in Benghazi, Libya, on Sunday news shows bordered on the actions of a lunatic fringe.

McCain's dustup was with a CNN producer over his missing a Capitol Hill briefing on Benghazi, a meeting that he, US Sen. Dianne Feinstein, and others had appropriately requested. McCain refused to answer a question on why he had no comment when queried about missing the briefing and then said: "I have the right as a senator to have no comment and who the hell are you to tell me I can or cannot?"[1] Three-time Pulitzer Prize–winning journalist, author, and Middle

East expert Thomas Friedman got it right when he said: "Libya is not a scandal, it's a tragedy. It's a story of an incredibly courageous ambassador who wanted to work with people on the ground and who produced something we have not seen since the Arab uprising, which is masses of Libyans on their own coming out to defend and praise our ambassador."[2]

In those simple and eloquent remarks, he sounded far more statesman-like than either McCain or Graham. US senators are supposed to behave like statesmen, rather than acting like cranky old men chasing kids off their front lawns. They have garnered too much respect over a career of noble public service to spend their remaining years on the public stage as little more than cantankerous, ill-tempered solons. Is adult, professional behavior too much to expect from a Navy war hero and an Air Force Reserve JAG officer? I think not.

In the present atmosphere of great distrust, rancor and often open hostility among our elected leaders, let us hope we can someday return to a previous period in American politics when civility, mutual respect and even, yes, honest friendships reigned, as exemplified by the genuine respect between President Ronald Regan and House Speaker 'Tip' O'Neill. Real leaders are able to find ways to compromise and put the people's welfare above their own.

30.
Leadership Takes a Village

G reat leaders have a vision and the capacity to motivate others to follow. Great leaders view the field from the mountaintop. Great leaders have the ability to inspire others but not be the center of attention themselves. Great leaders learn from the ups and downs of life experience.

As a society, we are fascinated with leadership and leaders. Great leaders reflect our innermost hopes and beliefs and, at their best moments, exhibit qualities we hold dear: valor, intelligence, hard work, tenacity, trust, honor, judgment, and dedication to a great cause.

To me, the question is not so much what makes a great leader but where we will find them going forward. It is a question that Lee Iacocca asked in his bestselling book *Where Have All the Leaders Gone?* and was reflected in the observation of one of the nation's leading experts on the topic, Noel M. Tichy of the University of Michigan School of Business, when he called leadership "the scarcest asset we have in the world right now."[1]

Where I live in Ventura County, California, efforts continue to evolve to ensure that the county produces people prepared to lead. The Ventura Chamber of Commerce, in conjunction with the United Way, has sponsored the Leadership Ventura program for more than a decade. The Resource Center at the Ventura County Community Foundation operates multiple programs year-round to assist board and executive leadership development throughout the county's large nonprofit sector. What is your community doing to promote leadership?

At California Lutheran University, I taught a business course in leadership, leveraging the knowledge and experience I gained through leadership training at the US Naval Academy at Annapolis, where I served as a Blue & Gold Officer, and as part of the Leadership San Francisco program sponsored by the city's chamber of commerce.

These and other efforts taking place throughout the county can make a difference. But there is a craving for effective leadership and more must be done to identify and cultivate this notion. It is time for those in a position of impact to demonstrate leadership themselves and abide by John Wooden's belief that "leadership is the ability to get individuals to work together for the common good and the best possible results while at the same time letting them know they did it themselves."[2]

Business, government, and education leaders would do well to follow more of the leadership traits explored in Robert Greenleaf's book *Servant Leadership* and understand that we all have a responsibility to help identify, develop, and groom tomorrow's leaders.[3]

City and county government and locally based companies need to help train recent graduates, share their expertise with nonprofit boards, and develop better leadership training programs within their own organizations if they want to prosper in the future. Colleges and universities need to come together in a true spirit of cooperation to form a Leadership Institute through which we can develop, nurture, and cultivate tomorrow's leaders. The public and private sectors need to join together to form leadership incubators to ensure that we remain a country that is both a wonderful place to live and work— while remaining competitive in a global economy. These are seeds we need to sow now if we hope to harvest the bounty later on.

Tichy said: "The individuals and organizations that build Leadership Engines and invest in leaders developing other leaders have a sustainable competitive advantage."[4]

"The most important task of an organization's leader is to anticipate crisis. Perhaps not to avert it, but to anticipate it."

—Peter F. Drucker

SECTION V

Why Branding and
Marketing Matter

31.
Brand Crusader in Chief

So your organization is contemplating a major brand or reputation initiative to increase competitiveness in today's sputtering economy. You are not alone in your leadership decision; however, finding counsel in publications or among a field of advisers or consultants can often amount to an exercise in frustration. Being at loggerheads over whether to call it reputation enhancement, brand management, or image building is as inane as watching the weather report on most Southern California evening newscasts. But that's exactly what reputation specialists, branding consultants, and academic purists often do in thinly parsing the differences. Such debates are much like wrangling over Camembert or Brie. Therefore, I will use the terms "reputation" and "brand" interchangeably as they go hand-in-hand from my 30-plus years of experience.

It almost goes without saying that achievement of positive brand image can be both elusive and fleeting, making return on investment a risky proposition. In today's competitive, increasingly global, and often unpredictable marketplace, any indiscretion of character or slipup in integrity—real or perceived by others—or major product defect can seriously jeopardize the company's reputation, image, brand, and success. BP, Goldman Sachs, Toyota, HP, and News Corporation come to mind immediately. Small businesses, though often considerably less insulated than multinational corporations, are at even greater risk of irreparable damage.

I've been privileged in my career to work with several organizations that have enviable brands. They include the US Navy and Marine Corps, Stanford University Medical Center, Blue Shield of California, the University of Michigan, the San Francisco Giants Baseball Club, the US Naval Academy, St. Joseph Mercy Health System, Pomona College, the University of California, and others. A common thread that unites these "best and brightest" is their insistence that everyone associated with the institution has a responsibility to uphold its reputation and that any major breaches are dealt with swiftly. They also impress upon all employees that brand messaging must penetrate every department and every employee must play a role in helping define and mold the company's brand.

Having been responsible for enhancing institutions' reputations and brands, I can assure you it is easier to mobilize employees around the need to strengthen an organization's brand than it is to engage them in the more esoteric concept of reputation. But for purposes of this discussion, let me assert what I believe is most important: that you take all the necessary steps to ensure your company's key constituencies are well aware of you, think highly of you, can accurately describe what you do, and are able to differentiate you from your rivals.

Having also served on and chaired a number of for-profit and nonprofit boards as a trustee, I have always believed that the CEO in particular must carry the banner, beat the drum, and set the example as the principal brand booster. In my book *Real Leaders Don't Boss* I describe examples of effective leaders and those who are less so. Real leaders ensure that branding is everyone's responsibility, but the CEO is its crusader in chief, supported enthusiastically by his or her executive team through whom management is held accountable.

A big part of your brand is how you are seen through the eyes of others. If an individual is dependable and hard-working, that is part of his or her brand. A company's brand instantly conveys a message; it creates a reaction in others that reveals how much they trust an organization and desire its products or services. Dr. Robert Sevier, senior vice president at Stamats, Inc., states that a brand is a promise made to customers.[1] Sevier, who has been a superb mentor to me over several years, makes a persuasive argument that a compelling brand gives an organization a competitive edge, one that competitors cannot often duplicate. Another leading brand expert, David Aaker, reminds us that a struggling brand often benefits by returning to its historical roots and rediscovering what made it thrive initially (for example, the Wells Fargo stagecoach, GE and its Thomas Edison days, and Hewlett and Packard's garage).[2]

Businesses in general—along with their leaders—must commit to heightening their reputation. To attain and enhance a reputation worth having, leaders must value integrity and character in themselves and others, and they must demonstrate now more than ever that their companies are enviable corporate citizens. As the 2012 Global Corporate Reputation Index uncovered, however, less than stellar contributions to one's community undermine companies' reputations.[3]

The Five Commitments to Reputation

1. Recommit to place core values ahead of the "win at any costs" mentality and manifest citizenship in clear, tangible ways.

2. Hire around your core values. In particular, pay attention to comprehensive and rigorous employee background checks to ensure that employees, management, and others connected with the organization are people of impeccable integrity.

3. Conduct initial training with new employees and regular ongoing training with existing employees on your core values, their meaning, and why they are important.

4. Make sure governing or controlling boards assert stronger leadership and oversight.

5. Commit to initiating more internal inquiries to strengthen compliance with rules and regulations.

Championing the Brand

In my career, I have worked in four distinct industries. In each field the best organizations believed that building a sustainable brand is about having a conscience and doing the right thing— and not necessarily because it garners good press.

As Sevier points out, the CEO must be the person to champion the brand because he or she alone is empowered to articulate the need for change, coalesce the executive team, redirect organizational funds as appropriate, and take the heat from one or more constituencies within the firm.[4] It is important that the CEO make the case for change convincingly if the organization is going to back a branding initiative.

But what happens if the branding mandate comes from a company's governing board or at the urging of a particularly important division from within and not from the C-suite? How can the branding initiative succeed under such circumstances? When a CEO or president provides only token support or lip service to a branding campaign, the executive team, management staff, and rank-and-file employees will quickly sense that their leader's heart is not really behind the campaign. This can severely hamper implementation.

If the president or CEO recognizes that his or her education, experience, or temperament does not directly contribute to the ability to articulate the case for the branding or rebranding initiative, but is following the board's wishes, the following must happen:

- Time must be devoted to prepare the CEO, helping him or her become more comfortable about lending his or her voice to branding in key meetings.

- The CEO must be given a funds reallocation plan he or she can present to the executive team to gain their support.

- The CEO must be encouraged and supported by the board chair and marketing-savvy board members so he or she doesn't feel out on a limb.[5]

Well before a branding initiative is launched, employees need to be thoroughly educated about the positive aspects of the changes and be made more aware of their competitive environment. Too many business leaders believe that if they have a marketing staff and marketing plans, branding will take care of itself. What they often have failed to consider is that the more emotionally connected consumers and employees are to the brand, the more effective every component of marketing becomes.

Especially when times are tough, products, markets, and industries are in constant flux. A well-managed, highly differentiated brand provides a discernible strategic direction and often an unarguable competitive advantage. And, as important as the executive team and employees are to the branding effort— and they are indispensible—the CEO must not relinquish his or her prime leadership role.

32.
Branding for the Long Run

Undoubtedly, one of the biggest words used in business today is "branding."

A brand encompasses many aspects of an organization and it instantly conveys a message. It creates a reaction in others that reveals how much they trust an organization and desire its products or services. A brand reflects an organization's reputation, standing, mission, and values. A brand is the promise we make to our customers.

In my own career, I have worked in four distinct fields and in each have been fortunate to have been the one executing or consulting for organizations that believed building a sustainable brand is about conscience and doing the right thing—and not necessarily because it garners good press.

It is widely believed that the CEO should be *the* person to champion the brand because he or she alone is empowered to articulate the need for change, coalesce the executive team, redirect institutional funds as appropriate, and "take the heat" from one or more constituencies within the organization. I believe it is important for the CEO to make the case for change convincingly if the organization is going to get behind the branding initiative.

What happens if the branding mandate comes from the governing board and not from the C-suite? How can the branding initiative succeed under such circumstances? The answer might be phrased "very carefully" because it takes much more patience, persuasion, and push. If the CEO or president gives only token support or merely provides lip service to a branding campaign, the executive team will quickly sense that his or her heart isn't really behind it, and everyone else will quickly come to the same conclusion, thus hampering implementation.

Organizations need to be adaptive in an environment that is constantly changing. In such a place, standing still is not a viable option. It takes constant refreshing and renewal for success in today's fierce global marketplace.

Clearly, not every organization is in a state of optimal readiness when the decision is made to engage in branding anew. So, how do you energize the organization, convincing employees to put their shoulders to the wheel?

Well before a branding initiative is launched, much work must have occurred in helping employees become more anticipatory. Everyone needs to be involved so they understand the purpose behind the rebranding effort. Former CEO of General Electric Jack Welch wrote: "Enthusiasm never hurts but real passion is sparked by purpose, by knowing why the organization is taking a certain path and what the journey will mean to them."[1]

Too many business leaders believe that if you have a marketing staff and marketing plans, branding will take care of itself. What they may not have considered is that the more emotionally connected employees *and* consumers are to the brand, the more effective every component of marketing becomes. Stephen King of the London-based WPP Group put it best when he said:

- "A product is something made in a factory; a brand is something bought by a customer.

- A product can be copied by a competitor; a brand is unique.

- A product can be quickly outdated; a successful brand is timeless."[2]

In the increasingly global world of business and education, products, markets, and industries are in constant flux. We would do well to remember that a well-managed brand provides a discernible strategic direction and an inarguable competitive advantage. And, as important as the CEO and the marketing team are to the branding effort, helping to conceive, execute, and protect the brand is every employee's responsibility.

In *A New Brand World*, Scott Bedbury writes that "all brands need good parents."[3] Similar to raising a child, building a brand takes at least 10 years of consistent care, nurturing, and support. But, it is worth the investment.

33.
What's in a Name?

Several examples both here in Los Angeles and around the nation underscore the intrinsic importance of choosing the right name for a company, organization, or institution. Just as parents don't haphazardly pick a name for a newborn son or daughter, so, too, the leaders of organizations need to marry logic with emotion in selecting the name for an emerging enterprise.

The Los Angeles landscape is dotted with many memorable names that have made their way into our collective culture: Mulholland Drive, Griffith Park, Grauman's Chinese Theatre, The Getty, the Hollywood Bowl, and Mt. Wilson among them. Sunset Boulevard became a classic film and the name Hollywood itself evokes dreams and fantasies in people around the world.

All of that brings us to the arts school dubbed Los Angeles Central High School No. 9 when it opened. My first thought was that the school board would have the wisdom to select a name that binds the rich heritage of the arts with the city in a way that tells a compelling story—and one that effectively builds on the history, tradition, and future of arts education.

Sadly, such forethought isn't always the case. In Washington, D.C., the Navy Department, apparently increasingly concerned about the prospects of defense cutbacks and wanting to curry political favor, announced plans to name an amphibious transport ship after the late Congressman John Murtha. Eschewing the tradition and system established in the early part of the 20th century of a system for choosing ship's names (in this particular classification of vessel that would have been American cities), one wonders about the appropriateness of naming a transport dock ship after a congressman. Having served in the Naval Reserve for nearly 30 years, I believe the Navy would be well served if it returned to the ship-naming custom established decades ago and avoid politicians altogether, with the exception of US presidents.

Likewise, in Indianapolis the merger of Indiana University Hospital, Methodist Hospital, and Riley Hospital for Children resulted in the made-up name of Clarian Health (more on this in the next chapter). As time proved, Hoosiers did not warmly embrace the invented name of Clarian, and as a result, hospital leadership renamed their hospital system with a name that is recognized and respected locally, regionally, and nationally: Indiana University Health.

Whether one is naming a school, a ship, a hospital system, or any other important entity, the name selected should meet the "Eight Be's" test:

1. Be distinguishing.

2. Be defining.

3. Be memorable.

4. Be descriptive.

5. Be a "force multiplier."

6. Be value added.

7. Be appropriate to the entity's location, role in society, and purpose.

8. Be a story that can be shared.

My great uncle has a school named after him in Roseville, California. Described as a gifted teacher and caring administrator, his name was deemed preferable to the lackluster Public School No. 5. as it perpetuates his legacy of leadership while encouraging both teachers and students to strive to live up to the high academic and public service expectations for which he stood. It resonated much more with the community than the au courant practice of naming schools after trees, streams, animals, and hills.

Selection of the right name can elevate an organization and make a lasting impression. It can foster enduring relationships and underscore the overall integrity of the entity. It also strengthens and emboldens those who already feel an emotional investment and, perhaps most important, builds authenticity, trust, knowledge, loyalty, imagination, and a moral high ground. Conversely, an ill-conceived name can doom that same organization to ridicule or obscurity.

What's in a name? Plenty. Just ask me to explain the importance of my boyhood idol's ballpark at UCLA, the Jackie Robinson Stadium!

34.
New Isn't Always Better

I was more than a little surprised when I learned the Indianapolis-based Clarian Health system planned to change its name to Indiana University Health. During the late 1990s, merger frenzy characterized US hospitals—the joint venture of Indiana University Hospital, Riley Hospital for Children, and Methodist Hospital of Indiana became official in January 1997 under a new name: Clarian Health.

Indiana University Hospital, Riley Hospital for Children, and Indiana University School of Medicine composed the IU Medical Center, where I served as the marketing, public relations, and hospital affiliations chief for nine years. When active discussions began about a possible IU–Methodist Hospital merger, the inevitable question arose about what this combined hospital system should be called.

Ritch K. Eich

As part of my role, my team and I assembled the latest market data, analyzed its findings, and developed a compelling set of recommendations for how to garner the most support possible for the new organization from its various constituencies—business leaders, physicians, and citizens across the state of Indiana.

I presented our recommendation to the interim leadership of the enterprise: Indiana University Health. Based on all the data we had collected, the existing equity in Indiana University's name, and the close alliance regional physicians felt toward the nation's second largest medical school, I made the case as strongly as I could that there was no more widely recognized or positively viewed name throughout the Hoosier state than Indiana University. Indiana University, frequently represented by the ubiquitous letters "IU," like all good brands stands for something—something vitally important to students, faculty, staff, alumni, organizations that hire its graduates, sports fans, and other constituencies alike. In a word, that something is called excellence. IU consists of eight campuses across the Hoosier state and enjoys a stellar worldwide reputation in research, teaching, and medicine as well as the humanities, the arts, and athletics. It is a powerful, widely known, and highly respected brand.[1]

Our recommendation wasn't accepted. Instead, the new hospital chain proceeded to spend thousands of dollars with an out-of-state consulting firm to develop a slate of "invented" names to brand the newly merged hospital system. The name "Clarian" was ultimately selected, and more dollars began to flow to create awareness for this newly coined moniker. (Webster must have been livid. Interestingly, the Clarion Hotel chain—using the correct spelling of the word—was also launched about that time.)

Nearly 15 years later in 2011, the leadership of Clarian Health decided to rename the system to—you guessed it—Indiana University Health. The feeling was that Indiana University Health would better identify Clarian's unique brand of nationally recognized healthcare, reinforce its partnership with Indiana University and the IU School of Medicine, and better reflect the breadth of its mission. They also hoped "to create a national brand, after the model of the Cleveland Clinic or the University of Pittsburg Medical Center."[2]

With reported annual revenue of $3.7 billion and a decade of acquisitions and rapid growth under their bigger belts, Clarian had the luxury of being able to spend additional tens if not hundreds of thousands of dollars in design, printing, signage, stationery, forms, badges, Web sites, direct mail, television and radio advertising, outdoor boards, clothing, and countless other materials required in establishing a new brand. They did it in 1997 and they did it again in 2011.

Through this process, Clarian learned a valuable lesson that CEOs, strategic planners, and marketers ought not to forget: Using an existing name (brand) when it is widely known, broadly accepted, and highly respected generates great customer and employee loyalty. It should be guarded, treasured, and respected.

35.
Branding Lessons from Law Schools

Not too long ago, the terms "branding" and "marketing" were anathema on many college campuses. Law schools were no exception. So when the invitation came to have lunch with the dean and a couple of trustees of the Santa Barbara and Ventura Colleges of Law to discuss a possible board seat, I was surprised—and not particularly interested in serving on another governing board. At last count, I'd served on more than a dozen boards of directors and chaired some of them.

I was informed that while the reputation of the Colleges of Law was strong among local attorneys and judges (and I later discovered during my due diligence that it was), its general awareness and recognition beyond legal circles were lacking, and would I consider helping them "turn that around"?

Most of the trustees of the Santa Barbara and Ventura Colleges of Law are sitting judges and practicing attorneys. To my pleasant surprise, they recognized to a person that rebranding the institution was not a frill but an absolute requirement in today's hypercompetitive and especially frugal business environment.

During the time I worked with them, the dean and trustees of the Colleges of Law recognized and embraced finding answers to all the right questions regarding the rebranding of the law school. A few of them are listed here:

- How much should we invest in rebranding the Colleges of Law?

- What is a realistic return on such an investment?

- How does branding fit within the overall law school strategic plan?

- How will the new brand differentiate us from other schools in the region?

- How do we enhance every encounter people have with the new brand and how do we clarify the brand "story"?

- What do our primary audiences think of the law schools?

- How will we ensure the new materials elevate our positioning in this market?

- How can we, as trustees, play a more visible, helpful role as the rebranding launch rolls out?

- How do we ensure that our online and print materials, collateral publications, and key messages complement our new brand?

- After we create a new visual identity, will we have a firm foundation of communication tools to inform future marketing decisions?

Like many organizations, the Santa Barbara and Ventura Colleges of Law is an institution "on the move." Armed with a new logo, a new catalog, increased media coverage, and a new Web site—all built around a new brand with strengthened visual aspects—the students, alumni, faculty, trustees, legal community and friends, and most important, prospective students will be impressed.

For students seeking a Juris Doctor degree that is affordable, convenient, part-time (thus enabling them to continue to hold their current job), and taught by highly respected lawyers and judges who bring real-world experience to the classroom, there is no comparable institution in the region.

As a former hospital executive, university administrator, and US Navy officer, I've worked with many outstanding civilian attorneys and JAG officers during my 30-plus-year professional career. Few of them, however, match the caliber of the judges and lawyers who sit on the board of the Santa Barbara and Ventura Colleges of Law. While I hope my leadership experience as well as my background in marketing and branding have been helpful to the law school, perhaps the greatest value trustees experience being part of a branding initiative are the following:

- Realizing that the primary audience or constituency of a law school's branding effort is neither the dean nor the faculty and board but rather prospective students. Understanding the impact that a brand can have on working professionals contemplating going to law school after work is paramount.

- Remembering that just as the practice of law and our court system continue to evolve, so too does the market in which the law school finds itself. Learning anew the needs, wishes, and wants of customers—prospective students—is essential, and they are the primary target audience of the new brand. I have often stated that while one hopes the administration, faculty, staff, and board of an educational institution embrace its new brand with enthusiasm, it is nonetheless even more important for them to endorse the more compelling goal: to excite, engage, and enroll prospective students.

An effective board of trustees wisely understands its need to perpetuate the mission and culture of its organization, to exercise its fiduciary responsibility but also to protect and heighten its new brand. As former Disney CEO Michael Eisner said: "A brand is a living entity and is enriched or undermined cumulatively over time, the product of a thousand small gestures."[1]

36.
Reputation as Brand

With increasing frequency, universities around the country are recognizing that their reputation and their brand are two of their most important, yet in many ways most intangible assets.

Having a good reputation has a positive influence on all the goals a university may set—from attracting top-notch students and faculty to meeting fundraising targets, fostering a strong alumni base, and nurturing strong town-gown relationships. It can influence public policy and, perhaps most important, enable the university to weather a crisis.

A good reputation goes hand in hand with a university's brand, which in essence is the promise that the institution makes to all of its constituencies. A brand reflects an organization's unique personality, distinguishing characteristics, and the reason for people to care. A strong university brand should permeate all corners of the campus—from academics to athletics to arts—and survive long after posters and pep rallies have faded into distant memory.

In many ways, both the reputation and the brand are hidden assets that, as in any other organization, can give a university a distinct competitive advantage on many fronts—if properly managed. However, while these attributes are crucial to success, they are highly vulnerable in today's era of competition, cynicism, and microscopic media scrutiny.

Both reputation and brand translate into how an individual or organization is seen through the eyes of others. For universities and colleges, these others include community leaders, current and future students, alumni, donors, faculty, legislators, the business community, competing colleges, the media, and any other group with whom the institution may interact or wish to impact. A good reputation will positively reflect what these constituents think of a university's academic merit, leadership team and management style, position in the market, social accountability, financial stewardship, physical campus, and sustainability over time.

Like any organization, a university's reputation is earned, not bought, and it is based on four imperatives. First, an organization must perform consistently over time. Strong, positive reputations are not created through clever slogans or expensive advertising campaigns. Those techniques may help to reinforce a university's reputation or brand once it is securely entrenched, but people will look at performance of the university and its leadership to be consistent, steady, and unfaltering to know if its promise is true.

Second, organizations must build an internal culture that supports and fosters the overall reputation it wishes to convey. This involves hiring faculty and staff who, beyond their core technical competencies or scholastic letters, have the ability to foster the university's reputation in a positive way. It also involves a leadership team whose management style is reputation focused and an internal communications program of accountability and candor that breeds such thinking.

Third, like other organizations, universities with durable reputations are those that understand and cherish the value of branding and refuse to do anything that strays from their brand's promise. They know that a properly managed brand helps support the university's reputation by accurately and consistently conveying key attributes that stand the test of time.

Finally, universities with the strongest reputations are invariably those that are values based and believe fervently that trust, honesty, and integrity are crucial concepts that cannot be compromised even in trying times. How an organization responds in its darkest moments of crisis will have a far more telling effect on its long-lasting reputation than what it does when the sun is shining.

A university with a good reputation—one based more on action than words—understands that it must never sacrifice principles or values for short-term gain or for the purpose of evading discomforting conflict.

Where I live, we are fortunate to have within our midst many outstanding and well-intentioned universities, including the University of California, Santa Barbara, Westmont College, Pepperdine, California State University, Channel Islands, and California Lutheran University. Each of these institutions has an intrinsic advantage over other industries because people inherently want to believe that universities are places where good deeds are being done, good values are being taught, and good leaders are being readied to emerge.

37.
The Importance of PR

Scandal and controversy are not new to organizations, including those in the healthcare world. Still, one would be hard-pressed to find any era as damaging to the reputation of hospitals and health systems as a whole as the one that began with the Columbia/HCA disgrace and continues right through today. The reputation "hits" range from Medicare fraud and dumping of indigent patients out on the street to transplant patients receiving the wrong organ and life-threatening inefficiences in the emergency department. As technology and burgeoning social media have made it far easier to uncover and spread damaging information, it is time to take a fresh look at how an organization handles its public image and what it can do to proactively build and maintain a strong reputation.

New practices like ethics training, anonymous reporting hotlines, and improved leadership development are good ways to prevent dangerous or illegal practices. Conflict of interest statements help, too, and greater transparency in decision making is also a part of the answer. But the problem goes even deeper than these methods can penetrate. Executive-level corruption has been the most damaging, and one answer may lie in a different way of thinking about executive supervision. That begins with an organization's board of directors.

Over the years, I have worked with many CEOs whom I have urged to seek professionals grounded in marketing and public relations to sit on their boards. And while it may not be uncommon for a marketing expert to hold this position, public relations expertise is largely unrepresented. This is probably because PR is generally considered to be "softer" and not as measurable as the effects of marketing that have traditionally been linked more closely with sales and quantitative accountability. As a result of this perception, the importance of PR expertise and the value it can bring are overlooked. The adage "if you can't measure it, it's not there" has unfortunately become a widely adopted misconception concerning the importance of PR to a company's bottom line.

While some PR-savvy counselors have gained seats at the table, too few boards of trustees have an experienced, skilled PR practitioner filling that role. It is this kind of omission that has kept many otherwise good institutions from seriously considering how potential scandal could damage their reputation and bring the CEO down from the inside.

A board needs someone trained in ethically protecting a company's image—someone who is experienced at putting out fires with minimum damage when necessary. Even more important, it needs a person who can help rein in and counsel executives before a crisis occurs. Highly skilled PR craftsmen are able to build effective relationships with a company's public and often serve as a company's alter ego, representing the community voice in an unfettered way. Ensuring accurate and transparent communication and relations with the public is an important PR skill that should not be ignored or neglected.

Having a leader with substantial experience in both marketing and PR on a board reinforces the importance organizations should attach to the role of reputation management as it relates to performance and public trust. Professionals who are trained and seasoned in marketing or PR can offer sound strategic advice when it comes to building a brand, growing trusted relationships with the media, and developing competitive market strategy (including product development, pricing, and market segmentation). Few other professions bring this portfolio of skills to the table.

A Harris Interactive study revealed that organizations can mitigate negative economic trends by greater sincerity and accuracy in their communications. An Institute of Market-Based Management study further confirmed the importance of reputation in lowered procurement costs, reduced risk of litigation, as well as enhanced recruitment and retention of talent. Their message is clear: It is a mistake to underestimate the value of trust and public image.

It is time for organizations to recognize that their reputation and trust within the community *are* its bottom line. With this understanding, public relations must play a far more significant role. As we navigate through crises of conscience, a new approach is needed, one that starts at the top and provides the capacity to address problems before they occur and before it is too late to mitigate the damage.

38.
The "Special" in Special Events

H istorically speaking, there have been two rather divergent views about the appropriate role of special events in business, politics, and the not-for-profit world. One perspective suggests that a special event is an end in and of itself, that it exists to achieve a one-time goal—introduce a new product, raise money, or commemorate a new facility. Another view, the one I advance, is that a special event is a means to a larger end— relationship building and reputation enhancement—for the longer term.

Special events, when properly conceived, managed, and leveraged to their fullest, are a very important part of an organization's overall reputation-building strategy. They can help to engage existing allies, attract new partners into the tent, create a forum for supporters new and old to share enthusiasm, and provide wonderful input for positive media coverage.

To be most effective, special-event coordination must be considered part of an organization's overall brand marketing mix. Viewing it as such ensures consistency in both message and timing with other marketing tactics such as direct mail, advertising, media relations, publications, and online navigation, content, and design. The best way to ensure all of these elements work in concert—that is, to maximize the potential of each and deliver optimal return on investment—is to have all these functions well coordinated and effectively led.

Sadly, special events are not always given their just due when it comes to the impact they can have and role they can play in an organization's overall reputation enhancement agenda. All too often, special events are treated as frills, and events coordinators are not seen as key members of a team. Even senior officers—who recognize the need for a "family look" to unify publications— rarely insist that events reflect the same discipline and continuity of purpose. Instead, they treat special events as independent, unrelated events. This is a huge mistake and undermines the many contributions that special events can bring to an organization.

As extensions of the institution's brand, special events can bring a community together, change an institution's image, or enhance existing messages. They can provide valuable media exposure, help grow business, build enrollment, stimulate philanthropy, and foster good will in the community as well as internally. Some of the notable special events where I live include Senior Concerns'

Ultimate Dining Experience, Casa Pacifica's Angels Ball, Boys & Girls Club of Conejo and Las Virgenes Gala, CLU's Corporate Leaders Breakfast Series, and CSUCI's President's Dinner.

For an organization's key constituencies, special events can represent a turning point in its decision-making process. A special event may constitute the first personal contact with the organization. An event can be the catalyst for transforming a visitor's abstract interest into tangible appreciation. The well-planned and well-executed event can convert a fence sitter into an advocate or a passive board member into an active one. Events can make vague concepts come to life or help instill pride. On the other hand, weak events can discourage constituents from wanting to learn more, if not drive them away altogether. One way or the other, special events represent critical junctures in the reputation enhancement process.

Enlightened business leaders realize that staging a special event takes much more than a dream or wish. It takes hundreds, sometimes thousands of hours of preparation. Whether large or small in nature, an event must be guided by a skilled organizer (and volunteers depending on the event) who is a combination of marketer and business leader capable of ensuring that the event's goals—along with budget parameters—are achieved.

This person must also understand that ultimately the event must be consistent with the mission, spirit, and image of the organization. The most brilliantly designed and executed special event will be counterproductive if its message is confusing or inconsistent with the institution's other activities—or if no strategy is included to follow up on the relationships formed during the event. Most important, special events must be seen as relationship and reputation builders.

"To lead people, walk beside them."

—*Lao-Tsu*

SECTION VI

Leaders Lead, Bosses Boss

39.
10 Tips for Business Success

In a time of significant upheaval in corporate America, climbing the corporate ladder may be quite different from what was even a few years ago. Vast changes in the workplace have made corporations as we know them flatter and more nimble, with employees located offsite as well as in office towers and many working part-time. The very nature of work may have been altered forever by economic crisis, increased technology, and globalization.

At a time when the income disparity in the United States is among the highest in the world, when people are finding it difficult keeping jobs or finding good fulltime jobs, and when executives of large companies are under attack from all sides, how does one approach the idea of advancement?

Having worked for many years in the upper ranks of leadership, served on corporate boards, and reported to many different board chairs, presidents, and CEOs, I found that working in leadership roles requires not only special skills but also different attitudes and approaches.

Here is a list of my 10 stepping stones learned through personal experience that anyone interested in climbing the corporate ladder should internalize:

1. *Always do a superior job.* This is obvious but worth restating. I have seen many would-be climbers who are not as interested in their own job duties as they are in other positions; this is a mistake. The first CEO I reported to told me that the most important task was doing a superior job with the duties I was given. "If you do that," he said, "the rest will soon fall into place."

2. *Evaluate new ideas carefully.* Thinking outside of the box must be rethought. Creative problem solving should be your best tool in a challenging business climate. However, an article published in 2011 by Knowledge@Wharton (University of Pennsylvania) found that new ideas are often perceived negatively in the workplace, and that "those who think outside the box may be penalized for it."[1] Therefore, innovators should evaluate new ideas carefully for viability, communicate the benefits in terms that people can understand and rally around, and be willing to do the work. In short: Respect the system and people who work within it. As Linda Hudson, CEO of

BAE Systems (US) commented in a 2011 interview, "It's better to work with the system from the inside" than to fight it.[2]

3. *Advance for the right reasons.* When opportunity knocks, look before you leap. Not all career advancements will be right for you, so before taking one, be sure you want it for the right reasons. Investigate some openings, but not all, and don't make a pastime of it, losing your focus. In her article "Female CEOs: What It Takes to Climb the Corporate Ladder," Tisa Silver comments that management positions are a good bet because "they show willingness to accept increasing responsibility and can foster leadership skills."[3]

4. *Expand your circle of colleagues.* Continually expand your nexus of friends, associates, and advisers. We learn from others' experiences and perspectives, so it is vital to continuously keep in contact with others, never forgetting to thank them for whatever help they give you. Mondelez International CEO Irene Rosenfeld tells women in her organization to "look for someone to speak on your behalf—like a sponsor who can put your name in the right place at the right time."[4]

5. *Develop future leaders.* Give a helping hand to those who show promise. I learned from several CEOs the importance of developing a pipeline of future leaders, something I have tried to do throughout my career. It is essential for success, and is also one of the most rewarding

duties I have known: to watch and help others grow and succeed.

6.   *Put the organization and its people first, not yourself.* The CEOs I admire most know this instinctively and practice it diligently. They have a laser-like focus on people and results, but never forget the importance of the role their associates play in the overall success of the enterprise.

7.   *Never stop learning.* A 2009 Corporate Internet Executive Research Study found "CEOs are reporting that their jobs are now requiring a huge array of skills and expertise."[5] And on the list of top 10 women CEOs compiled by Tisa Silver, all 10 had their four-year degree and six had postgraduate degrees. Working on any type of advanced professional education or certificate program shows others that you are serious about your career and willing to go the extra mile for it.

8.   *Explore other parts of your organization.* Shadow human resource colleagues in meetings when appropriate, and spend some time in manufacturing or with sales and marketing staff in the field. By understanding other divisions, you are expanding your value to the firm and your overall knowledge of how the business works.

9.   *Develop your global outlook.* Moving up may well require relocation, and your chances increase with your willingness to accept a position that takes you far from home. Stephen Green, CEO at HSBC, defines a global

attitude as "having a passion and curiosity about the world" and "a willingness to accept good ideas no matter where they come from." He says, "No one gets to the top at HSBC without having worked in more than one market," and that HSBC executives are hired with the expectation that they will be very mobile.[6]

10. *Keep a positive attitude.* Lastly, don't allow yourself to be influenced by those who are petty, backstabbing, cruel, or worse. Remain positive in your focus and don't lose your sense of humor.

A wise person once said, "Many an opportunity is lost because a man is out looking for four-leaf clovers." Despite all the change and volatility in corporate America, never forget that career advancement remains inextricably linked to the basic principles of organizational performance.

40.
Knowing When It's Time
to Move On

O n the morning of December 12, 1941, just five days after the attack on Pearl Harbor, newly minted Brigadier General Dwight D. Eisenhower was summoned from Texas to meet with Army Chief of Staff General George Marshall. He was directed to present Marshall with a strategy within just a few hours to lead to victory in the Pacific. Without delay, Eisenhower drafted a three-page memo outlining his strategy. His action is illustrative of one of the most important leadership tools too seldom used in marketing today—strategy.[1]

Executives, managers, and others in transition (for example, many of President Obama's first-term marketing campaign staffers) need a personal strategy to guide them in their careers. Their strategy should have benchmarks by which they can judge whether the time is nearing for them to move on in their careers and not overstay their welcome.

Successful healthcare marketers typically possess a strong strategic bent, substantial conceptual skills, an engaging personality, and proven analytical ability. Yet few seemingly deploy personal strategies in their own careers. According to executive search firm SpencerStuart, chief marketing officers across all industries average just 45 months in a particular job.[2] This relatively short tenure suggests that marketers would definitely benefit from a strategy to guide them in their professional pursuits.

Marketing professionals must be able to discern when the time has come to leave behind a comfortable, challenging, or captivating job—however difficult that may seem. Knowing when it's time to say goodbye is a sensibility that's often lacking. A career strategy can help immensely.

Robben Fleming told me one afternoon when he was about five years into his job as president of the University of Michigan that he decided a decade was a "pretty good rule of thumb," as it enables leaders to accomplish most of their goals and hopefully avoid "wearing out one's welcome." Fleming left the university to become president of the Corporation for Public Broadcasting 10 years after he arrived in Ann Arbor. Like Eisenhower, Fleming served in World War II and clearly grasped his mission. He had an overarching strategy to succeed and the requisite skills to ably guide the university during the turbulent Vietnam War years of student protests.

When you as a marketing vice president, director, or manager feel the need to make a career move, chances are your instincts are probably correct. Even when close friends or family members may not perceive your instincts as logical or strategic, it doesn't mean they are not valid.

Achieving most of the goals you originally projected is an excellent benchmark for coming to terms with a timetable to move on. But there are other cogent reasons for doing so. Here are a few:

- You have become seduced by the trappings of success.

- The relationship with your supervisor is in a downward spiral.

- Your skills have begun to erode.

- Your organization has become increasingly unreceptive to your ideas.

- You have become isolated from key constituencies.

- It's become increasingly difficult to alter your course quickly.

- The organization's culture is not in sync with your principles.

- You seem to have lost your passion and vision.

The truth is that people look for new career opportunities for many reasons, and they differ with each individual. Whatever the situation, keep in mind five key guidelines about leaving a job and settling into a new one successfully:

1. *Don't burn your bridges.* Keeping relationships at your previous employer intact may help you in many ways in the future, especially if you plan to stay in the same industry.

2. *Leave something important behind you.* Leave something you can be especially proud of and not simply something to put on your résumé. Doing so will contribute to your own sense of purpose.

3. *Take the lessons you learned and apply them to your new situation.* Remember that your new job is not your old one and be open to a new environment and new ways of doing things. You have great skills to bring with you, but they will be used in a different context, so don't expect people and situations to be the same. Learn the lay of the land before instituting too many changes.

4. *Be friendly and respectful to all the new people you meet.* Wherever you go, some people will see new hires as a threat. Treating everyone respectfully will help you earn the trust and support you need and will let people see you as a welcome member of the team. Be open, receptive, and forge an honest working environment.

5. *Challenge yourself to learn fresh skills.* Your new position offers the opportunity to contribute to your organization in important state-of-the-art ways to bolster its competitive advantage.

When you confront the question of whether the time has come to move on, perhaps Ralph Waldo Emerson's words of wisdom will help:"To map out a course of action and follow it to the end, requires some of the same courage which a soldier needs."[3]

AFTERWORD

STEP UP TO THE PLATE
Insights, Thoughts, and Ideas to Help You Hit a Home Run

- Don't hide your passion. Sharing your enthusiasm can be contagious, and make a real difference.

- Don't make things harder by complaining constantly and being unreasonably demanding—whether you are dealing with your boss or your team. Instead, focus on being a problem solver—your efforts will most likely lead to greater responsibilities and future promotions, and your team will go to bat for you.

- Don't forget to roll up your sleeves and work alongside your team—your actions promote collaboration and cooperation, allow you to see how your team interacts, and provide you with a great opportunity to be a mentor and coach.

- Encourage cross-training so that everyone is ready to pitch in when needed. Cross-training also provides people with the opportunity to lean a new skill, and can be a lifesaver if there's an extended period of time between someone leaving and a replacement being hired.

- It should go without saying that after completing a project successfully, recognize everyone (and I do mean everyone) who contributed.

- Don't be afraid of hiring someone because you feel they might outshine you—their accomplishments will reflect well on you.

- Be available to your team when *they* need you. You may be inconvenienced at times, but respect is reciprocal and your accessibility shows that you respect them, and that they are important to the organization.

- Establish and promote an environment where everyone feels safe, valued, and empowered to contribute—this includes keeping an open mind and listening. Identify input that is actionable, act on it, and always give credit where it is due.

- Make an effort to get to know your colleagues from across the organization—you'll be surprised at what you can learn by meeting with coworkers from other departments, divisions, or affiliates within your organization. By understanding the role others play in your organization, you increase your own knowledge base—and value. It never hurts to have friends in other parts of the organization.

- Don't overlook "small wins" by only focusing on just home runs. Stretch goals are fine, but your team needs to feel they are achievable and that you aren't asking them to perform the seemingly impossible. Singles and doubles can add up over the long term, and build energy, momentum, and trust along the way.

- Take responsibility, and don't blame others for your own mistakes. One of the surest ways to demoralize your team is to blame them for something that isn't their fault. Own up to your mistakes, focus on lessons learned, and rededicate yourself to future efforts.

- Leadership is about serving others, not yourself. The very best leaders check their egos at the door, are humble, and love to teach, support, and encourage their teams—especially during difficult economic times. As someone once told me, "Watch out for those who smile up the organization and frown down the organization."

- Read voraciously and never stop learning. If you constantly seek to expand your intellectual and creative boundaries, you will become a much more knowledgeable, valued, interesting, and sought-after employee.

- It may seem passé in an era of texting and digital shorthand to fine-tune your writing skills. But being an effective communicator means being able to write clearly, succinctly, and thoughtfully. You will enhance your organization's reputation—as well as your own—more than you realize.

- Never be afraid to seek assistance from others, but choose carefully. Most of us are flattered when asked to help a new or a more experienced team member. In my experience, the best leaders make time to mentor others who are interested in being mentored.

- Develop your own philosophy of leadership—have a clearly defined system of beliefs and practices and use them regularly, but not rigidly. Convey your philosophy consistently to your team. You can always expand your philosophy as you gain more experience and more knowledge but resist fads, so-called gurus, and "quick fix" experts.

- Be confident in your own abilities and beliefs but beware of yes-men and women. As stated above, don't be afraid to hire people smarter than you and to listen to them—while sticking to your principles.

- Expect to fail—it is an invaluable experience. As stated previously, learn from your mistakes, and move forward with greater wisdom and resolve.

- Leadership development is a journey. Like baseball, it encompasses many innings and a strong team. There is no one-size-fits-all answer that works for every situation. By experiencing the crucibles along the way, you'll come out stronger, more resilient, and more valuable—to the organization and yourself.

Play ball!

NOTES

Chapter 1

1. Ronald Reagan used this Russian proverb during negotiations with Soviet General Secretary Gorbachev in Reykjavik, Iceland, October 11–12, 1986.

2. Max DePree, *Leadership Is an Art* (East Lansing, MI: Michigan State University Press, 1987).

3. Stephen M. R. Covey, *The Speed of Trust* (New York: Free Press, 2008).

Chapter 2

1. *The Holy Bible,* English Standard Version (Wheaton, IL: Crossway, 2001).

2. *The Holy Bible,* New King James Version (Nashville, TN: Thomas Nelson, 1982).

3. Warren G. Bennis and Robert J. Thomas, *Geeks & Geezers* (Boston: Harvard Business School Press, 2002).

4. Tony Zinni and Tony Koltz, *Leading the Charge: Leadership Lessons from the Battlefield to the Boardroom* (New York: Palgrave Macmillan, 2009).

5. Attributed as an African proverb, origin unknown.

Chapter 3

1. Attributed to Peter Drucker, but no original source was found.

2. Rebecca Leung, "The Mensch of Malden Mills," *60 Minutes,* video, CBS News, February 11, 2009.

3. Albert Einstein, letter to Morris Raphael Cohen, professor emeritus of philosophy at the College of the City of New York, defending the appointment of Bertrand Russell to a teaching position, March 10, 1940.

Notes

Chapter 4

1. Oliver Wendell Holmes, Memorial Day speech in Keene, NH, May 20, 1884.

Chapter 5

1. "University of Miami asks for 'corrupted' NCAA investigation to end," *SI.com*, April 4, 2013.

2. Warren Buffett, "Stop Coddling the Super Rich," *New York Times,* August 14, 2011.

Chapter 6

1. Robert Andrews, *Concise Columbia Dictionary of Quotations* (New York: Columbia University Press, 1989).

Chapter 7

1. John P. Kotter, *A Sense of Urgency* (Boston: Harvard Business School Publishing, 2008).

2. Noel M. Tichy and Eli Cohen, *The Leadership Engine* (New York: HarperCollins, 1997).

3. Ibid.

Chapter 9

1. Ken Blanchard and Spencer Johnson, MD *The One Minute Manager* (New York: William Morrow and Company, 1981).

Chapter 10

1. Dennis Sparks, "Explain, Inspire, Lead: An Interview with Noel Tichy," *JSD* 26, no. 2 (Spring 2005), 50, http://www.learningforward.org/docs/jsd-spring-2005/tichy262.pdf?sfvrsn=2.

2. Dan Ciampa, "Almost Ready," *Harvard Business Review,* January 2005.

Notes

3. B. L. Ochman, "Survey: Only 2% of Execs Write Their Own Blogs, That's Simply Dishonest!" *What's Next? Blog,* January 4, 2006, http://www.whatsnextblog.com/2006/01/survey_only_2_of_execs_write_t/.

4. Joseph Ellis, *American Sphinx: The Character of Thomas Jefferson* (New York: Random House, 1996).

5. Egon Zehnder, "Interview with General Colin Powell," *The Focus Magazine,* May 2006.

6. Larry Bossidy and Ram Charan, *Execution: The Discipline of Getting Things Done* (New York: Random House, 2002).

Chapter 11

1. Scott Monty, "Ford CEO: 14 Lessons in Leadership & Marketing," *The Social CMO Blog*, February 13, 2010, http://www.thesocialcmo.com/blog/2010/02/ford-ceo-14-lessons-in-leadership-marketing.

Chapter 12

1. Howard Engel, *The Man Who Forgot How to Read* (New York: St. Martin's Press, 2007).

Chapter 13

1. Warren Bennis and Patricia Ward Biederman, *Organizing Genius* (Reading, MA: 1997), 77. Bennis mentions that "he understood the wisdom of an observation that Xerox's chief scientist and PARC advocate Jack Goldman had clipped from a newspaper and hung in his office" and he then discusses this quote at http://freedomincbook.com/2011/07/02/warren-bennis-on-how-leaders-can-be-creative/.

Chapter 14

1. Herb Kelleher, "Business of Business is People," *YouTube video* (October 14, 2008).

Notes

Chapter 15

1. Rich DeVos, *Ten Powerful Phrases for Positive People* (New York: Center Street, 2008).

2. Pat Williams and Tommy Ford, *Bear Bryant on Leadership* (Saratoga Springs, NY: Advantage Press, 2010).

3. DeVos, *Ten Powerful Phrases for Positive People*.

Chapter 17

1. Barry Levinson, "The Band That Wouldn't Die," *30 for 30,* video, ESPN documentary series, October 13, 2009.

2. Nancy Coey, *Finding Gifts in Everyday Life* (Raleigh, NC: Sweetwater Press, 1995).

Chapter 18

1. Sonia Sotomayor, "Presidential Reception for Justice Sonia Sotomayor," C-Span Video Library, August 12, 2009.

2. Stephen H. Norwood and Harold Brackman, "Going to Bat for Jackie Robinson: The Jewish Role in Breaking Baseball's Color Line," *Journal of Sport History* (Spring 1999). Much information on this topic was culled from 1947 writings of Wendell Smith, confidant and friend of Jackie Robinson who wrote for the *Pittsburgh Courier*, an African-American newspaper, and from Jackie's own autobiography. Writer Dan Burley's writings were also used.

3. Ronald Heifetz, Alexander Grashow, and Marty Linsky, "Leadership in a (Permanent) Crisis," *Harvard Business Review* (July 2009).

Chapter 20

1. Dan Senor and Saul Singer, *Start-Up Nation: The Story of Israel's Economic Miracle* (New York City: Hachette Book Group, 2009).

Notes

Chapter 22

1. Emmet John Hughes, *The Ordeal of Power: A Political Memoir of the Eisenhower Years* (New York City: Atheneum, 1963).

Chapter 23

1. Palmer Morrel-Samuels, "The National Benchmark Study: Employee Motivation Affects Subsequent Stock Price," paper presented at the annual meeting of the American Psychological Association, Toronto, Canada, August 2009.

Chapter 25

1. Bo Schembechler, locker room speech to University of Michigan football team in 1983.

2. Dave Brandon, interview with author, May 24, 2011.

3. Jim Vesterman, "From Wharton to War," *Fortune Magazine,* June 8, 2006.

4. John C. Maxwell, "Create a Winning Team," *Success Magazine,* May 3, 2011.

Chapter 27

1. John P. Kotter, *A Sense of Urgency* (Boston: Harvard Business School Publishing, 2008).

2. Noel Tichy and Eli Cohen, *The Leadership Engine* (New York: HarperCollins, 1997).

3. Ibid.

Chapter 28

1. Karl E. Weick, "Small Wins: Redefining the Scale of Social Problems," *American Psychologist,* January 1984.

2. George L. Kelling and James Q. Wilson, "Broken Windows: The Police and Neighborhood Safety," *The Atlantic,* March 1982.

3. Cynthia Reynolds, *Jiffy: A Family Tradition* (Chelsea, MI: Chelsea Milling Company, 2008).

4. Niccolo Machiavelli, *The Prince* (New York: Mentor Books, 1952).

Chapter 29

1. John McCain, reply to CNN reporter Ted Barrett in the halls of Congress, November 15, 2012.

2. Thomas Friedman, remarks on NBC News *Meet the Press,* November 18, 2012.

Chapter 30

1. Jim Amidon, "Leadership Starts with Integrity," *Wabash Magazine,* Summer/Fall 2003.

2. John Wooden and Steve Jamison, *Wooden—A Lifetime of Observations and Reflections On and Off the Court* (Chicago: Contemporary Books, 1997).

3. Robert Greenleaf, *Servant Leadership* (New York: Paulist Press, 1977).

4. Noel Tichy and Eli Cohen, *The Leadership Engine* (New York: HarperColins, 1997).

Chapter 31

1. Robert A. Sevier, *Building a Brand That Matters* (Hiawatha, IA: Strategy Publishing, 2002).

2. David A. Aaker, *Brand Portfolio Strategy* (New York: Simon & Shuster, 2004).

3. Global Corporate Reputation Index is a study of 6,000 companies from six countries based on 40,000 consumer interviews by such nationally recognized reputation and branding companies as Burson-Marsteller, Landor Associates, Penn Schoen Berland, and BrandAsset Consulting. Citizenship is an umbrella for a host of cause-related, volunteer,

philanthropic, crisis response, sustainability, and other measures provided by businesses to help those individuals and nonprofit organizations in need around the globe.

4. Robert A. Sevier, numerous discussions with author over several years.

5. Robert A. Sevier, *Integrated Marketing for Colleges, Universities and Schools* (Washington, DC: CASE, 1998). See also White Papers produced by Robert A. Sevier and colleagues at Stamats, Inc. (www.stamats.com) and Robert A. Sevier, *An Integrated Marketing Workbook* (Hiawatha, IA: Strategy Publishing, 2003).

Chapter 32

1. Jack and Suzy Welch, "Emotional Mismanagement," *BusinessWeek,* July 16, 2008.

2. Judie Lannon and Merry Baskin (eds.), *A Master Class in Brand Planning: The Timeless Works of Stephen King* (West Sussex, England: John Wiley & Sons, 2007).

3. Scott Bedbury, *A New Brand World* (New York: Penguin Group, 2002).

Chapter 34

1. I was privileged to serve at Indiana University Medical Center for nine years and traveled extensively throughout the Hoosier state and contiguous states.

2. J. K. Wall, "Clarian Hospital System to Adopt IU Name," *Indianapolis Business Journal,* May 5, 2010. See also Shari Rudavsky, "Clarian Employees Swept Up in Rebranding," *Indianapolis Star,* December 12, 2010.

Chapter 35

1. Michael D. Eisner with Tony Schwartz, *Work in Progress* (New York: Hyperion, 1998).

Chapter 39

2. Knowledge@Wharton, "A Bias against 'Quirky'? Why Creative People Can Lose Out on Leadership Positions," *Leadership and Change,* February 16, 2011, http://knowledge.wharton.upenn.edu/article.cfm?articleid=2713.

3. Beth Kowitt, "BAE's Linda Hudson: How to Climb the Corporate Ladder," *CNNMoney.com*, March 15, 2011.

4. Tisa Silver, "Female CEOs Who Climbed the Corporate Ladder," *Investopedia.com,* March 18, 2012.

5. Irene Rosenfeld, Q&A at Catalyst Awards Conference, New York City, March 29, 2011.

6. "2009 Corporate Internet Executive Research Study," *Internet Strategy Forum,* http://www.internetstrategyforum.org/research/.

7. C. K. Prahalad, Rosabeth Moss Kanter, and Lawrence H. Summers (eds.), "In Search of Global Leaders," *Harvard Business Review on Leadership in a Changed World* (Boston: Harvard Business Review Press, 2004).

Chapter 40

1. Thomas E. Ricks, *The Generals* (New York: Penguin Group, 2012).

2. SpencerStuart, "Chief Marketing Officer Tenure Now at 45 Months," news release, May 1, 2013.

3. Widely attributed to Ralph Waldo Emerson, but no original source found.

RESOURCES

Aaker, David A. *Brand Portfolio Strategy*. New York: Simon & Shuster, 2004.

————. "Leveraging the Corporate Brand." *California Management Review*, Spring 2004.

Abrashoff, D. Michael. *It's Our Ship*. New York: Business Plus, 2008.

Allen, Judy. *Event Planning*. Etobicoke, Ontario: John Wiley & Sons, 2003.

Alsop, Ron. *The Trophy Kids Grow Up*. San Francisco: Jossey-Bass, 2008.

Amidon, Jim. "Leadership Starts with Integrity." *Wabash Magazine*, Summer/Fall 2003.

"Armed Forces: Zinging Zumwalt, U.S.N." *Time Magazine*, November 9, 1970.

Badaracco, Joseph L., Jr. *Leading Quietly*. Boston: Harvard Business School Press, 2002.

Baker, William F., and Michael O'Malley. *Leading with Kindness*. New York: AMACOM, 2008.

Balboni, John. *Lead with Purpose*. New York: AMACOM, 2012.

Barner, Robert. *Bench Strength*. New York: AMACOM, 2006.

Bedbury, Scott. *A New Brand World*. New York: Penguin Group, 2002.

Bennis, Warren. *On Becoming a Leader*. Reading, MA: Addison-Wesley, 1989.

Bennis, Warren, and Patricia Ward Biederman. *Organizing Genius*. Reading, MA: Addison-Wesley, 1997.

Bennis, Warren, and Burt Nanus. *Leaders*. New York: HarperCollins, 1985.

Bennis, Warren, and Robert J. Thomas. *Geeks and Geezers*. Boston: Harvard Business School Press, 2002.

————. *Harvard Business Review on Developing Leaders*. Boston: Harvard Business School Press, 2004.

Resources

Benton, D. A. *How to Think Like a CEO*. New York: Warner Books, 1996.

Bergman, Barrie. *Nice Guys Finish First*. Self-published, 2009.

Betof, Ed. "Leaders as Teachers." *T+D*, May 2004.

Blanchard, Ken, and Spencer Johnson, MD. *The One Minute Manager*. New York: William Morrow and Company, 1981.

Bossidy, Larry, and Ram Charan. *Execution: The Discipline of Getting Things Done*. New York: Random House, 2002.

Bracey, Hyler. *Building Trust: How to Get It! How to Keep It!* Self-published, 2002.

Brokaw, Tom. *The Greatest Generation*. New York: Random House, 1998.

Bryant, Adam. "He Wants Subjects, Verbs and Objects." *New York Times,* April 26, 2009.

Brzezinski, Mika. *Knowing Your Value*. New York: Weinstein Books, 2011.

Brzezinski, Zbrigniew. *Strategic Vision: America and the Crisis of Global Power*. New York: Basic Books, 2012.

Buffett, Warren. "Stop Coddling the Super Rich." *New York Times*, August 14, 2011.

Cannon, Jeff, and Jon Cannon. *Leadership Lessons of the Navy Seals*. New York: McGraw-Hill, 2003.

Charan, Ram. *Leadership in the Era of Economic Uncertainty*. New York: McGraw-Hill, 2009.

Choudhury, Uttara. "Wharton's Leadership Program Is at the Heart of MBA Life." *Braingainmag.com*, July 16, 2011.

Ciampa, Dan. "Almost Ready." *Harvard Business Review*, January 1, 2005.

Coey, Nancy. *Finding Gifts in Everyday Life*. Raleigh, NC: Sweetwater Press, 1995.

Resources

Cohen, Eli, and Noel Tichy. "How Leaders Develop Leaders." *Training & Development*, May 1997.

Collins, Jim. *Good to Great*. New York: HarperCollins, 2001.

———. *How The Mighty Fall*. New York: HarperCollins, 2009.

Conaty, Bill, and Ram Charan. *The Talent Masters*. New York: Crown Business, 2010.

Covey, Stephen M. R. *The Speed of Trust*. New York: Free Press, 2006.

Crockett, Roger O. "How P&G Finds and Keeps a Prized Workforce." *BusinessWeek*, April 9, 2009.

Deal, Terrence E., and Allen A. Kennedy. *Corporate Cultures*. Reading, MA: Addison-Wesley, 1982.

Denove, Chris, and James D. Power, IV. *Satisfaction*. New York: Portfolio, 2006.

DePree, Max. *Leadership Is an Art*. New York: Currency, 1989.

———. *Leadership Jazz*. New York: Currency, 1992.

DeVos, Rich. *Ten Powerful Phrases for Positive People*. New York: Center Street, 2008.

Drucker, Peter F. *Managing the Non-Profit Organization*. New York: HarperCollins, 1990.

———. *The Effective Executive*. New York: HarperCollins, 2002.

———. "The American CEO." *Wall Street Journal,* December 4, 2004.

Egon Zehnder. "Interview with General Colin Powell." *The Focus Magazine*, May 2006.

Eisner, Michael D., and Tony Swartz. *Work in Progress*. New York: Hyperion, 1998.

Engel, Howard. *The Man Who Forgot How to Read*. New York: St. Martin's Press, 2007.

Ellis, Joseph. *American Sphinx: The Character of Thomas Jefferson.* New York: Random House, 1996.

Erskine, Carl. *What I Learned from Jackie Robinson.* New York: McGraw-Hill, 2005.

Erwin, Dan. "Why Is Defense Secretary Gates So Successful?" *Dan Erwin* (blog), February 9, 2010.

Farnham, Alan. *Forbes Great Success Stories.* New York: John Wiley & Sons, 2000.

Gagne, Matt. "A Fine Vintage." *Sports Illustrated,* February 7, 2011.

George, Bill. *True North.* San Francisco: Jossey-Bass, 2007.

Gerstner, Lewis V., Jr. *Who Says Elephants Can't Dance.* New York: HarperBusiness, 2002.

Goethals, George R., Georgia J. Sorenson, and James MacGregor Burns. *Encyclopedia of Leadership,* Vols. 1-4. Thousand Oaks, CA: Sage, 2004.

Goldblatt, Joe Jeff. *Special Events: Best Practices in Modern Event Management.* New York: John Wiley & Sons, 1997.

Goulston, Mark, and John Ullmen. *Real Influence.* New York: AMACOM, 2013.

Greenleaf, Robert K. *Servant Leadership.* Mahwah, NJ: Paulist Press, 1977.

Harari, Oren. *The Leadership Secrets of Colin Powell.* New York: McGraw-Hill, 2002.

Harvard Business Review on Developing Leaders. Boston: Harvard Business School Press, 2004.

Heifetz, Ronald A. "Leadership in a (Permanent) Crisis." *Harvard Business Review,* July 2009.

Heifetz, Ronald A., Alexander Grashow, and Marty Linsky. *The Practice of Adaptive Leadership.* Boston: Harvard Business Press, 2009.

Resources

Herdt, Timm. "Ex-Gowen Man Credited with Saving Infant's Life." *Ventura County Star,* December 16, 1992.

Hesselbein, Frances, Marshall Goldsmith, and Richard Beckhard. *The Leader of the Future.* San Francisco: Jossey-Bass, 1996.

Howard, Carole M., and Wilma K. Mathews. *On Deadline.* Prospect Heights, IL: Waveland Press, 2000.

Hoyle, Leonard H. *Event Marketing.* New York: John Wiley & Sons, 2002.

Hughes, John Emmet. *The Ordeal of Power: A Political Memoir of the Eisenhower Years.* New York: Atheneum, 1963.

Iacocca, Lee. *Where Have All the Leaders Gone?* New York: Scribner, 2007.

Issacson, Walter. *Steve Jobs.* New York: Simon and Shuster, 2011.

Kahn, Roger. *The Boys of Summer.* New York: HarperCollins, 1987.

Kelleher, Herb. "Business of Business Is People." *YouTube video,* October 14, 2008.

Kelling, George L., and James Wilson. "Broken Windows: The Police and Neighborhood Safety." *The Atlantic,* March 1982.

Kennedy, Caroline. *Profiles in Courage for Our Time.* New York: Hyperion, 2002.

Kennedy, Edward M. *True Compass.* New York: Twelve, 2009.

Knowledge@Wharton. "A Bias against 'Quirky'? Why Creative People Can Lose Out on Leadership Positions." *Leadership and Change,* February 16, 2011. http://knowledge.wharton.upenn.edu/article.cfm?articleid=2713.

Komisarjevsky, Chris. *The Power of Reputation.* New York: AMACOM, 2012.

Kotter, John P. *A Force for Change.* New York: The Free Press, 1990.

———. *A Sense of Urgency.* Boston: Harvard Business Press, 2008.

Kouzes, James M., and Barry Z. Posner. *The Leadership Challenge.* San Francisco: Jossey-Bass, 2007.

Resources

Lafley, A. G., and Ram Charan. *The Game-Changer.* New York: Crown Business, 2008.

Lannon, Judie, and Merry Baskin. *A Master Class in Brand Planning: The Timeless Works of Stephen King.* West Sussex, England: John Wiley & Sons, 2007.

Laymon, Rob, and Kate Campbell. "Learning to Lead, Marine Style." *Wharton Alumni Magazine,* Summer 2001.

Lemons, James. "Richard L. Schreiner, M.D." Remarks, IUPUI Retiring Faculty Recognition Luncheon, Indianapolis, IN, May 3, 2011.

Levinson, Barry. "The Band That Wouldn't Die." *30 for 30.* Video. ESPN documentary series. October 13, 2009.

Lowney, Chris. *Heroic Leadership.* Chicago: Loyola Press, 2003.

Lowry, Rich. "Jackie Robinson's Achievement." *National Review Online,* April 16, 2013.

Lucas, James R. *The Passionate Organization.* New York: AMACOM, 1999.

Lutz, Bob. *Icons and Idiots: Straight Talk on Leadership.* New York: Portfolio/Penguin, 2013.

Machiavelli, Niccolo. *The Prince.* New York: Mentor Books, 1952.

Manning, George, and Kent Curtis. *The Art of Leadership.* Boston: McGraw-Hill, 2003.

Maxwell, John C. *The 21 Indispensable Qualities of a Leader.* Nashville, TN: Thomas Nelson, 1999.

———. *The 17 Essential Qualities of a Team Leader.* Nashville, TN: Thomas Nelson, 2002.

———. "Create a Winning Team." *Success Magazine,* May 3, 2011.

McGrath, Rita Gunther. *The End of Competitive Advantage.* Boston: Harvard Business Review Press, 2013.

Resources

Mcllvaine, Andrew R. "GE Opens the Doors to Crotonville. *" Human Resource Executive Online,* November 23, 2009.

"Nation: Humanizing the U.S. Military." *Time Magazine*, December 21, 1970.

Norwood, Stephen H., and Harold Brackman. "Going to Bat for Jackie Robinson: The Jewish Role in Breaking Baseball's Color Line." *Journal of Sports History*, Spring 1999.

Ogilvy, David. *Ogilvy on Advertising*. New York: Vintage Books, 1985.

Oliver, Vicky. *Bad Bosses, Crazy Co-Workers & Other Office Idiots*. Naperville, IL: Sourcebooks, 2008.

O'Reilly, Charles A., III, and Jeffrey Pfeffer. *Hidden Value*. Boston: Harvard Business School Press, 2000.

Orfela, Paul, and Ann Marsh. *Copy This!* New York: Workman Publishing, 2005.

Ornstein, Norman J. "Ted Kennedy: A Senate Giant, Partisan Hero and Legislative Master." *Roll Call,* May 21, 2008.

Pfeffer, Jeffrey. *What Were They Thinking?* Boston: Harvard Business School Press, 2007.

Prahalad, C. K., Rosabeth Moss Kanter, and Lawrence H Summers (eds.). "In Search of Global Leaders." *Harvard Business Review on Leadership in a Changed World*. Boston: Harvard Business Review Press, 2004.

Reina, Dennis S., and Michelle L. Reina. *Trust & Betrayal in the Workkplace*. San Francisco: Berrett-Koehler Publishers, 1999.

Reynolds, Cynthia Furlong. *"Jiffy" A Family Tradition*. Chelsea, MI.: Chelsea Milling Company, 2008.

Ricks, Thomas E. *The Generals: American Military Command from World War II to Today*. New York: Penguin Press, 2012.

Resources

Ries, Al, and Laura Ries. *The 22 Immutable Laws of Branding*. New York: HarperBusiness, 2002.

Robbins, Stephen P., and Timothy A. Judge. *Organizational Behavior*. Upper Saddle River, NJ: Pearson, 2009.

Robinson, Jackie. *I Never Had It Made*. New York: Rachel Robinson, 1972.

Rucker, Philip. "Kennedy's 'Farm System' Now Wields Power." *Washington Post*, August 28, 2009.

Sandberg, Sherly. *Lean In*. New York: Alfred A. Knopf, 2013.

Schembechler, Bo, and John U. Bacon. *Bo's Lasting Lessons*. New York: Business Plus, 2007.

Schwartz, Larry. "Jackie Changed Face of Sports." *ESPN.com*, October 10, 2002.

Senor, Dan, and Saul Singer. *Start-Up Nation: The Story of Israel's Economic Miracle*. New York: Hachette Book Group, 2009.

Sevier, Robert A. *Thinking Outside the Box*. Hiawatha, IA: Strategy Publishing, 2001.

———. *Building a Brand That Matters*. Hiawatha, IA: Strategy Publishing, 2002.

———. *An Integrated Marketing Workbook*. Hiawatha, IA: Strategy Publishing, 2003.

Slater, Robert. *Jack Welch & the G.E. Way*. New York: McGraw-Hill, 1999.

Smith, Chad "Corntassel." *Leadership Lessons from the Cherokee Nation*. New York: McGraw-Hill, 2013.

Sparks, Dennis. "Explain, Inspire, Lead: An Interview with Noel Tichy." *National Staff Development Council*, Spring 2005.

Spencer Stuart. "Chief Marketing Officer Tenure Now at 45 Months." News release, May 1, 2013.

Resources

Sotomayor, Sonia. "Presidential Reception for Justice Sonia Sotomayor." C-Span Video Library. August 12, 2009.

Spiegelman, Paul. *Why Is Everyone Smiling?* Dallas, TX: Brown Books, 2007.

Sutton, Robert I. *The No Asshole Rule.* New York: Warner Business Books, 2007.

———. *Good Boss, Bad Boss.* New York: Business Plus, 2010.

The Holy Bible. English Standard Version. Wheaton, IL: Grossway, 2001.

The Holy Bible. King James Version. Nashville, TN: Thomas Nelson, 1982.

Tichy, Noel M. "GE's Crotonville: A Staging Ground for Corporate Revolution." *The Academy of Management EXECUTIVE* III, no. 2 (1989).

Tichy, Noel M., and Warren G. Bennis. *Judgment: How Winning Leaders Make Great Calls.* New York: Portfolio, 2007.

Tichy, Noel M., and Eli Cohen. *The Leadership Engine.* New York: Collins Business Essentials, 2007.

Thompson, William. *Gumption.* Self-published, 2010.

Vogel, Steve. "Saluting the Admiral Who Steered the Navy." *Washington Post,* January 11, 2000.

Walsh, Bill, Steve Jamison, and Craig Walsh. *The Score Takes Care Of Itself.* New York: Portfolio, 2009.

Weick, Karl E. "Small Wins: Redefining the Scale of Social Problems." *American Psychologist,* January 1984.

Weick, Karl E., and Kathleen M. Sutcliffe. *Managing the Unexpected.* San Francisco: Jossey-Bass, 2001.

Weiss, Alan. *"Good Enough" Isn't Enough.* New York: AMACOM, 2000.

Weiss, Kenneth R. "No Longer the University of Second Choice." *Los Angeles Times Magazine,* September 17, 2000.

Resources

Welch, Jack. *Winning.* New York: HarperCollins, 2005.

Welch, Jack, and Suzy Welch. "Emotional Mismanagement." *Business Week,* July 16, 2008.

Wharton, Clifton R., Jr. "Reflections on Leadership, Diversity and Human Capital." Speech delivered at the American Agricultural Economic Association Annual Meeting, July 26, 2005.

Whitehead, Don. *The Dow Story.* New York: McGraw-Hill, 1968.

Williams, Pat, and Tommy Ford. *Bear Bryant on Leadership.* Saratoga Springs, NY: Center Street, 2008.

Wisconsin Leadership Institute. "Old vs. New Forms of Leadership." *Wisconsin Leadership Institute,* July 2011.

Woodall, Marian K. *Thinking on Your Feet.* Bend, OR: PBC, 1996.

Wooden, John, and Steve Jamison. *Wooden: A Lifetime of Observations and Reflections On and Off the Court.* Chicago: Contemporary Books, 1997.

Zenger, John H., and Joseph Folkman. *The Extraordinary Leader.* New York: McGraw-Hill, 2002.

Zinni, Tony, and Tony Koltz. *Leading the Charge: Lessons from the Battlefield to the Boardroom.* New York: Palgrave Macmillan, 2009.

ACKNOWLEDGMENTS

During the past 30 years I have had the good fortune of knowing, working with, meeting, or closely following the careers of a large, diverse stable of leaders from practically every sector of society. They range from board chairs and CEOs to publishers, editors, and reporters; from civil servants and military personnel to entrepreneurs and academics; and from clergy and insurers to athletic directors and coaches. They all share one distinguishing quality: they give unselfishly of their time, knowledge, and experience. They personify what Peter Drucker meant when he wrote: "No one learns as much about a subject as one who is forced to teach it."

This book, *Leadership Requires Extra Innings*, is my second book, following *Real Leaders Don't Boss* (Career Press, 2012). Like my first book, proceeds from its sale will be donated to charity. In this case, proceeds will be donated to the Jackie Robinson Foundation, a national not-for-profit organization founded by Rachel Robinson, Jackie's widow. I hope in some small way its contents will encourage readers to seek increasingly challenging growth experiences, apply insights from those life lessons, and thereby become more successful leaders.

Almost all of the essays in this book were published previously, and I would like to acknowledge and thank the following for kindly allowing me to include them here, in some cases in their original form and in some cases updated:

Los Angeles Business Journal: Chapter 33. Reprinted with permission of the Los Angeles Business Journal.

Modern Healthcare: Chapter 26. Reprinted with permission from the July 4, 2011, issue of *Modern Healthcare.* © 2011 Crain Communications Inc. All rights reserved.

Monster.com, Workforce Management: Chapter 27. Copyright 2013. This article first appeared in the Monster Resource Center. Visit Hiring.Monster.com. You may not copy, reproduce or distribute this article without the prior written permission of Monster Worldwide, Inc. All Rights Reserved.

Pacific Coast Business Times: Chapters 1, 2, 5, 10, 14, 17, 22, 23, 32, 35, 39. Reprinted with permission of the Pacific Coast Business Times.

Santa Barbara News Press: Chapter 36. Reprinted with permission of the Santa Barbara News Press.

Strategic Healthcare Marketing: Chapters 34, 37, 40. Reprinted with permission of Health Care Communications.

Ventura County Star: Chapters 3, 4, 6–9, 11-13, 15, 16, 18–21, 25, 28–30 38. Reprinted with permission of the Ventura County Star.

I wish to sincerely thank the following people who helped me in countless way in the preparation of this book: Gary Ames; Larry Ames; John G. Argo; Tod Bannister; Laurie Barkman; Eugene A. Bauer, MD; Ken Beachler; Warren Bennis; Ryan Bjork; Connie

Acknowledgments

Blaszczwk; Gregory Blesch; Elise Bogdan; Michael Bradbury; David Brandon; Sarah Hardesty Bray; William Campbell; Samuel Coto; Mike Craft; Charles Crumpley; Dale Carnegie Training Corporation; Rich DeVos; Henry Dubroff; Dianne Easton; Harold Edwards; Amy Ellwood; Jim Estill; RADM Jim Finkelstein, USN (ret); Jeff Folks; Dave Francis; Vince Galloro; Elizabeth Gingerich; Ross Goldberg; Rabbi Mark Golub; Steve Grafton; Howard S. "Howdy" Holmes; Sevanne Kassarjian; Bill Kearney; and Carol Keochekian.

Also, Allison Krieger; Jim Kristie; Cathryn Kulat; Diane Kuntz; Amy Levin-Epstein; Dennis McCafferty; Mike McCurry; Lauren Melesio; Michael Mink; John T. Moore; Mary Olson; Les Palm; Tony Peck; Dr. Ora Pescovitz, MD; Bill Plaschke; Aaron Rogers; Lou Saalbach; Martha Sadler; Markus Schuler; Christopher Scott; Ken Shelton; Laura M. Smith; Steve Stumpf; Raymond Sun; Noel Tichey; Michael Todd; Emmanuel Touhey; John Ullmen; Mark VanderKlipp; Marlize van Romburgh; Michele von Dambrowski; Clifton R. Wharton, Jr., PhD, and Mrs. Dolores D. Wharton; Will Wlizlo; and Tess Woods.

I had the pleasure of working with several great teams of people including the Medical Center Relations team at Indiana University Medical Center: Mary Minix, Lynaire White, Kathryn Alexander, Jan Michelson, Mary Maxwell, Kathleen Hopper, Brian Kelley, Suzie Mathis, Pam Perry, Karen Alter; and others.

Others' works have positively influenced most authors I know. I am no exception. The following people have written articles, books, and monographs and given speeches that I have found both inspiring and influential: Ron Alsop; Gary Armstrong; Dan Beckham; Warren Bennis; Mika Brzezinski; Zbigniew Brzezinski; Ram Charan; Jim Collins; Bill Conaty; Stephen M. R. Covey; Mike Craft; Max DePree; Rich DeVos; Peter Drucker; Henry Dubroff; Bill George; Ross Goldberg; Philip Kotler; John Kotter; James Kouzes; Jim Kristie, A. G. Lafley; Larry Lauer; Susan Marks; John C. Maxwell; John T. Moore; Burt Nanus; Charles O'Reilly III; Jeffrey Pfeffer; Bill Plaschke; Barry Posner; Gen. Colin Powell, USA (ret); Jackie Robinson; Rachel Robinson; Sheryl Sandberg; Robert Sevier; Ken Shelton; Robert Sutton; RADM William Thompson USN (ret); Noel Tichy; Clifton R. Wharton, Jr., PhD; Jack Zenger; and other distinguished authors.

I have had the privilege of working directly with many organizations that have published my work, written about me, or assisted me in other ways. Their representatives have been helpful, insightful, and patient with me and have frequently suggested improvements to my submissions for which I am very grateful. They, too, have been excellent "teachers" and include the following publishers, publications, and other organizations: Career Press; Communication Quarterly; Corbin Design; Costco Connection; Diane Kuntz Design; Directors and Boards; Leadership Excellence; Leadership San Francisco; Los Angeles Business Journal; Los Angeles Daily News; Los Angeles Times; Marine Corps Gazette; Michigan State University and its alumni association; Modern Healthcare; Monster.com; Pacific Coast Business Times; Pacific Standard (formerly Miller-McCune Magazine); Payers & Providers; Sacramento State University, its athletics department, and its alumni association; Sales and Service Excellence; Santa Barbara Independent; Santa Barbara News Press; Stanford University Report; Strategic Health Care Marketing; The Hill; The Journal of Values-Based Leadership; The Thousand Oaks Acorn; Thomas Nelson Publishing, Brazil; Trusteeship Magazine and AGB; University of Michigan, its athletics department, and the alumni association; University of Michigan Libraries (and their incredibly talented, resourceful, and responsive reference librarians); US Naval Institute and Proceedings Magazine; and Ventura County Star. I am sure there are others I have not included and for that, I extend my apologies—and my gratitude.

Throughout the process of preparing *Leadership Requires Extra Innings*, I have been extremely fortunate to have the expertise, savvy, and guidance of Cynthia Zigmund, president of Second City Publishing Services, LLC. And, thanks to Cynthia's intrepid spirit and unwavering commitment to seeing this project through, no deadlines were missed. I also want to commend my superbly talented graphic designer, Diane Kuntz of Diane Kuntz Design, who conceived the book cover. I would be remiss if I didn't acknowledge the eleventh hour assistance of my copyeditor, Jack Kiburz, and my good friends, Mark VanderKlipp, president of Corbin Design, and Ross Goldberg, president of Kevin Ross Public Relations, who were also most helpful.

My wife of 44 years, Joan Taylor Cummings, is the love of my life, my Rock of Gibraltar, and my most candid and, therefore, most helpful critic. Our sons, Geoff and Ted, and our daughters-in-law, Nancy and Mary, are already impressive leaders in their respective professions. And, stand by for our grandchildren as Taylor Sun, John Patrick, Carter Jameson, and Caroline Elizabeth who, individually and collectively, are going to be a force with which to reckon. Their abiding love, strong encouragement, and keen interest have made it possible for me to go into "extra innings." I am blessed to be on such a winning team.

ABOUT THE AUTHOR

Dr. Ritch K. Eich has spent more than three decades studying the philosophies and fundamentals of true leaders. He's worked with or for a who's who of world leaders, from Howard Holmes (Jiffy Mix) to Tom Monaghan (Domino's Pizza founder) to Charles Walgreen, Jr. (Walgreen Drug Stores). Ritch is cofounder and president of Eich Associated, a strategic leadership, marketing, and communications consulting firm; an adjunct professor at California Lutheran University; a frequent speaker and blogger on leadership and marketing; and a former columnist for various business and professional publications. His first book, *Real Leaders Don't Boss: Inspire, Motivate, and Earn Respect from Employees and Watch Your Organization Soar,* was published in 2012 by Career Press.

Community service has always been an important part of Ritch's commitment to leadership development. He has served on the board of directors of the University of Michigan Alumni Association, an independent organization that serves approximately 500,000 alumni and friends of the university. Previously, he was also selected to join the board of trustees of the Santa Barbara and Ventura Colleges of Law and served on the board of directors of the Gold Coast Veterans Foundation and the advisory board of the Kingsmen Shakespeare Festival. Ritch is a past chair of the board of trustees of Los Robles Hospital and Medical Center and is a past member of Downtown Rotary in Ann Arbor and later in Indianapolis and the United Way. He was also a Pharmaceutical Research and Manufacturers Association

Fellow at Abbott Laboratories in Chicago. He is a captain, US Naval Reserve (ret) and commanded three reserve units.

Ritch believes fervently in giving back, and has served on the founding board of trustees of the University of California–Merced Foundation and on the founding boards of directors for the Ronald McDonald House of West Michigan and the USS Indianapolis Memorial. He served on the board of VCEDA (Ventura County Economic Development Association) and the University of Michigan Military ROTC Board, and is a graduate of Leadership San Francisco and the Stanley K. Lacy's Executive Leadership Association's Opportunity Indianapolis. He has enthusiastically provided his time, expertise, and gifts to countless organizations, some of which are pictured here.

Ritch served on the alumni board of the University of Michigan. Pictured here is the U-M Alumni Center. (Photo courtesy of Benjamin Logan of the U-M Alumni Association)

The Lilly House and Gardens, the historic 1930s home of J. K. Lilly, Jr., is on the grounds of the Indianapolis Museum of Art. Ritch and his team at IU Medical Center held many strategic planning "Advances" at the IMA, always finishing early so his staff could visit some of the more than 50,000 works of art there. (Photo courtesy of the IMA's Anne M. Young and Kristen Mullins, Ebby Grace Photography, Indianapolis)

Los Robles Hospital and Medical Center is where Ritch served on the board for several years, later chairing the hospital's board of trustees. (Photo courtesy of Kris Carraway-Bowman, Los Robles Hospital)

The Kingsmen Shakespeare Festival draws large crowds every summer to the bucolic campus of California Lutheran University. Ritch has served on the board of the festival for several years and was a champion of the fine and performing arts while serving as CLU's first vice president for marketing and communications. (Courtesy of Tim Hengst, Kingsmen Shakespeare Company)

Riley Hospital for Children, one of the main components of IU Medical Center—now called IU Health—is a wonderful organization that Ritch and his team served with great pride for nine years. (Courtesy of Kristen Mullins, Ebby Grace Photography, Indianapolis)

The Gold Coast Veterans Foundation, on whose board Ritch served, anticipates and responds to critically important needs presented by veterans from the Tri-Counties region of Southern California: Ventura, Santa Barbara, and San Luis Obispo. (Photo courtesy of JC Oberst)

Ritch served on the founding board of trustees of the University of California Merced Foundation. Ritch and his wife, Joan established the first Trustees' Scholarship on the campus. (Photo courtesy of Patti Waid, Office of Communications)

Ritch served on the founding board and raised private contributions to help create the USS Indianapolis Memorial, a tribute to the crew of the last capital ship sunk in WWII. When sunk, approximately 300 men went down with the cruiser and about 900 were left floating in shark-infested waters—316 were rescued four days later. The memorial was the 50-year dream of the survivors in honor of their missing shipmates. (Photo courtesy of Kristen Mullins, Ebby Grace Photography, Indianapolis)

One of Ritch's most rewarding experiences was helping US Navy Memorial founder RADM Bill Thompson, with fundraising and marketing strategy. The Lone Sailor statue pictured here in Bremerton, WA, is a copy of the original in Washington, DC. (Photo ©2012 Chris Davis)

Index

Index

Index

Index

Index

Index

Index

www.ingramcontent.com/pod-product-compliance
Lightning Source LLC
Chambersburg PA
CBHW022111210326
41521CB00028B/199